Michael T. Winstanley SDB

Alive!

The Gospel Resurrection Narratives: Then and Now

Don Bosco
Publications

Don Bosco Publications
Thornleigh House, Sharples Park, Bolton BL1 6PQ
United Kingdom

ISBN 978-1-909080-41-6
©Don Bosco Publications 2018
©Michael T. Winstanley SDB

Front cover photograph by Fr Michael T. Winstanley SDB

Printed in Great Britain by Jump Design and Print

For Frank Moloney SDB

Faithful friend and eminent scholar
In thanks and appreciation

Foreword

One of the most difficult of tasks in biblical studies is translating scholarly work on scripture into language that speaks vividly to Christians today. Not many have the capacity to effect the translation; it is a rare and fine gift when it can be found. Some authors write at a popular level that steers well clear of scholarly arguments. Others write at an academic level, their work full of jargon and analysis that is inaccessible (and probably uninteresting) to anyone outside the discipline. The gulf between the two means that most writing runs the risk of being, on the one hand, shallow and ill-informed or, on the other hand, impenetrable and verbose.

Michael's is a book well worth reading. Apart from anything else, it successfully and beautifully bridges the gap. Here is someone who knows the scholarship well and yet can articulate it in a readable way for the ordinary Christian who wants to understand the Gospels better.

The endnotes are thorough enough to give access to scholarly debate in clear, non-technical language. You gain a real sense of where the arguments lie and what they actually mean. Not everyone will necessarily want to read all the endnotes, but everyone will want to know that they are there. They demonstrate the knowledgeable and thoroughly researched basis from which the book is written. The same grasp of scholarly issues pervades not only the text and its endnotes but also the conclusion, which touches on the question of history and the resurrection accounts.

In bridging the gap between the scholarly and the popular worlds, the prose succeeds in being delightfully lucid. This is a writer who can really write, who has facility with English, who can communicate, who can weave metaphor and personal anecdote into his literary style. As a result, it is a pleasurable as well as instructive experience to read this book.

Sensitivity to the narrative itself is a real asset of the book. Michael understands how the resurrection stories are written in the Gospels, how they are shaped and structured, how the medium communicates the message. He takes the story dimension seriously without skimming over it or treating it as background. He immerses himself in it and enables you, the reader, to do the same.

But above all, the book is deeply theological—theological, not in the narrow of mere adherence to correct doctrine, but in the sense of bringing the core message of Jesus to life. Theology, in this view, is closely allied to spirituality. Michael makes wonderful connections between the Gospel narratives, their meaning and the contemporary reader in his or her experience. At the end of each chapter, there is a section called 'Reflections' where these points of connection to the reader's spiritual and pastoral experience are unfolded. They are immensely fruitful links and give rise to further reflection in the mind of the reader.

The core theology of the book is that the resurrection of Christ is "the world's transforming catalyst", as the introduction notes, offering hope and life in the places of human discouragement, despair and death. "The most amazing lesson of all is the revelation of love", says the chapter on John 21 which explores Jesus' challenge to Simon Peter, visible in both his forgiving of Peter's denial and his giving of major responsibility to him. In the resurrection "Jesus moved forward into a radically new and very different kind of life, beyond all the limitations of space and time", says the conclusion, showing how that life is given to us through the Spirit, not to hold to ourselves but to share with others.

As a woman engaged in ministry in the church, I was grateful for the acknowledgement of women's discipleship and their crucial role in the resurrection narratives and for the challenge to the Church today.

As a biblical scholar, I loved the way the book values and evaluates each Gospel in its uniqueness. There is no bland harmonising of the four Gospels here but a recognition that each Gospel has its own story, its own theology, its own connecting links to lived human experience. The differences are made plain, as well as the points of similarity, giving a sense of the diversity of the canon and the breadth of the Gospel witness.

Mark's Gospel, for example, is described as "breathless" and you immediately have the image of Mark the evangelist breaking open the Gospel story as he runs, proclaiming it in his hasty way through human loss and failure. Matthew's Gospel emphasises Jesus' teaching and presence, where through baptism we are "immersed in the bonds of family love binding the three and binding the members of the community". Luke's narrative of the journey to Emmaus is one of the most beautiful and affecting of the all the Gospel stories, an "exquisite masterpiece" of narrative and theology, leading the disciples from tragedy to hope and joy.

Two chapters are devoted to John's resurrection narratives, one focused on Jerusalem and the other on Galilee. By exploring the dramatic stories of Mary Magdalene, Thomas, Peter, the Beloved Disciple, and the gathered group of disciples, we gain a sense of how resurrection can transform our lives: from darkness to light, from doubt to faith, from chaos to peace, from failure to forgiveness.

In the end, as Michael reminds us, true aliveness for us as Christians comes in our relationship with the risen Christ who draws us into a deeper sense of awareness—of ourselves, of others, of the plight of the world—and into a responsiveness that is selfless and self-giving. We come to share more and more of Jesus' resurrection and its power to transform our lives and our world.

Dorothy A. Lee
Frank Woods Professor of New Testament
Trinity College
University of Divinity
Melbourne.

Contents

Copyright Acknowledgement

Introduction

Just over a year ago, at table during a celebration at Savio College, our Salesian school in Bootle, one of the guests made the suggestion or request that I should write a book on the resurrection. Having just completed 'Walking with Luke', I replied with a smile that another literary project wasn't on my agenda for the near future. However, a seed had been sown, and several invitations to deliver talks and study days on that subject began to nudge me in the direction of picking up the suggestion. This book is the result. I quickly realised that I already had quite an amount of material available in my files and in other books that I had written, so the task began to feel less daunting, and, in fact, quite exciting.

The title chosen for the book, 'Alive!', stems from two sources. First, I have for many years found the words of Jesus during the final meal with his disciples as told by John inspirational: "Because I am alive, you also will be alive" (14:19). The departure of Jesus through his being "lifted up" will not be the end of his story, nor of the story of his disciples. Jesus celebrates his being alive, and also its consequence, the aliveness of his disciples, an aliveness given a new dimension through the gift of the Spirit, an aliveness which is caught up in the life of God. For "on that day you will know that I am in my Father, and you in me and I in you" (14:20). We can have life in all its fullness (10:10). This, I believe, is what Christian spirituality is all about.

Secondly, one of the people whose memory I hold very dearly, a Salesian priest called Fr Harold Wrangham, frequently used to ask: "Who wouldn't be alive?" That question would be posed as we shared a glass of Croft Original sherry or examined the plants in the garden or the trees on the estate or were enjoying a meal with the community. By then he was well into his seventies, but still so vibrantly aware of the life within and around him. That question of his is one that I mull over frequently forty years on, especially as those years flow quickly by,[1] and I appreciate more than ever life's wonder and mystery.

In this book, therefore, I would like to explore what the Gospel resurrection narratives tell us about the aliveness of Jesus and its implications for our own aliveness, now and beyond the grave. Obviously, for us Christians, the resurrection of Jesus is absolutely foundational for our faith and spirituality.[2] As early as 54 CE, Paul, writing to the Christian community in Corinth, stated quite bluntly:[3] "If Christ has not been raised, then our preaching is in vain and your faith is in vain" (1 Cor 15:14).

The resurrection of Jesus is the world's transforming catalyst. It would seem that initially the belief of the early Christians in Jesus' resurrection was not articulated in the form of a written narrative; it was proclaimed in preaching, catechesis, liturgy, prayer and confessions of faith.[4] In the light of their experience of the risen Jesus, the disciples began to preach and proclaim him as Messiah, Saviour and Lord. They invited their hearers to accept the forgiveness he brought, to share the life of God which he made available, to experience salvation, to become part of his new community, God's new people. The fact of the resurrection, its meaning and implications, formed the core of their message. "'God raised him from the dead' is probably the earliest distinctively Christian affirmation and confession."[5]

The evidence suggests that simple phrases or formulas were used to articulate their deep faith conviction; these we find mainly in the letters of Paul. The basic one is: "Jesus is Lord." "No one can say 'Jesus is Lord' except by the Holy Spirit" (1 Cor 12:3). "If you confess with your lips that Jesus is Lord and believe in your heart that God raised him from the dead, you will be saved" (Rom 10:9). This is part of Paul's preaching and catechesis. In a liturgical hymn we find: "Therefore God also exalted him and gave him the name which is above every name, so that at the name of Jesus every knee should bend, in heaven and on earth and under the earth, and every tongue should confess that Jesus Christ is Lord, to the glory of God the Father" (Phil 2:9–11).

Some of these short formulas, sometimes referred to as two member/clause formulas, simply stated the basic Christian belief. Some of these statements were sequential, like "Jesus died and rose again" (1 Thess 4:14). Others were antithetical, stressing the contrast between the crucifixion or death of Jesus and his resurrection: "It will be reckoned to us who believe in him who raised Jesus our Lord from the dead, who was handed over to death for our trespasses, and was raised for our justification" (Rom 4:24). "Who is to condemn? It is Christ Jesus, who died, yes, who was raised, who is at the right hand of God, who indeed intercedes for us" (Rom 8:34). Similar formulas are also found in the sermons in Acts, for example: "… by the name of Jesus Christ of Nazareth, whom you crucified, whom God raised from the dead" (Acts 4:10; see 2:23–24; 5:30–31; 10:39–40).[6]

Sometimes the verb "lives" is used as an alternative to "raised": "He was crucified in weakness, but lives by the power of God" (2 Cor 13:4). "For to this end Christ died and lived again, so that he might be Lord of both the dead and the living" (Rom 14:9). His continuing to be alive is the result of his having been raised. Most expressions used the language of resurrection ("The One who raised Jesus from death" (Rom 8:11; 1 Cor 6:14; 2 Cor 4:14; Acts 2:24; 13:30)); other expressions adopted the language of exaltation or glorification, sometimes in early hymns: "God has highly exalted him" (Phil 2:9); "He ascended high above all the heavens" (Eph 4:10); "He was taken up into glory" (1 Tim 3:16).[7]

The idea of the resurrection of the dead was current among the Jews of Jesus' day, though the Sadducees did not accept it. But there were other models available: Elijah was thought to have been assumed into heaven (2 Kgs 2:1–12). The book of Wisdom speaks of immortality (3:1–8). It was not inevitable that resurrection language came to be used; it needs to be explained. Many Jews expected resurrection of the dead in the last times; but there was no expectation of the resurrection of an individual, separate from or preliminary to the general resurrection.[8]

A longer formula is found in Paul's first letter to the Christian community at Corinth.[9] This letter is usually dated as written in 54 or 56 CE. He probably founded the community in 50/51 CE. In this letter he quotes a formula which he says he learned in his early days as a Christian, so it could go back to the mid to late 30s. The full text reads:

> For I handed on to you as of first importance what I in turn had received: that Christ died for our sins in accordance with the scriptures, and that he was buried, and that he was raised on the third day in accordance with the scriptures, and that he appeared to Cephas, then to the twelve. Then he appeared to more than five

hundred brothers and sisters at one time, most of whom are still alive, though some have died. Then he appeared to James, then to all the apostles. Last of all, as to someone untimely born, he appeared also to me. (15:3–8)

As well as being very old, this is the only testimony we have which is written by someone who claims to have seen the risen Jesus. A few points are worth noting. The language of "hand on" and "receive" are technical terms for the handing on of a tradition. So it is a primitive tradition, and there is a formality about it. Scholars believe that the original formula probably ended after "appeared" or after the reference to "the twelve". Paul has added the rest.[10] The reference to "the scriptures" in both the first and third items is significant, reflecting the early Church's interest in exploring Old Testament background for what happened to Jesus. The sequence brings out the continuity in the story, which will be fleshed out later in the Gospel narratives.[11] This is the first reference to Jesus appearing, which is not mentioned in the shorter formulas; there is no attempt to localise what happened, and it is difficult to pinpoint exact chronology. The Greek verb can mean that Christ was seen, appeared, let himself be seen, showed himself; the initiative clearly lies with him.

Forty or fifty years later, the Gospel writers composed narratives to proclaim this good news.[12] Each evangelist used his own unique style, reworking early traditions according to his own theological vision and aims.[13] There are two basic traditions: in Matthew, Mark (by implication) and John 21, the main appearance of the risen Jesus to his disciples occurs in Galilee, whereas in Luke and John 20, it takes place in Jerusalem.[14] These Gospel stories have made such an impact on Christian belief and living over the centuries, and, I'm sure, on our own lives too. One writer comments that "the resurrection narratives in the Gospels are among the oddest stories ever written. At one level they are simple, brief and clear, at others complex and perplexing."[15] As well as the main appearances to the "twelve", there are narratives that describe the finding of the empty tomb, in two of which there is also an appearance of Jesus. In examining these narratives in this book, I shall adopt the following order: Mark, Matthew, Luke and John. Mark provides no Appearance Narrative, so we are restricted to his version of the finding of the empty tomb; for the other three evangelists, I shall explore the happenings around the tomb, and then the appearances.

In examining any Gospel passage, I believe it is useful and enriching to embrace a threefold approach: theological (what is the message, the word from God), literary (how is the message delivered as a piece of literature), and historical (what are the facts behind the message). Some of these resurrection narratives are brilliant pieces of literature; the evangelists are artful storytellers and show great literary skill, employing various techniques such as irony, symbolism, inclusion, parallelism. Historical issues are always fascinating and can exert a strong pull on our interest; we all wish to know what really happened. These issues I will touch on in the final chapter. But these narratives are not meant to provide biographical information or reconstructions of the events. Their main focus is theological; and it is this aspect and its impact on our spirituality that I wish to highlight and reflect on particularly.[16] These Gospel episodes are catechetical stories; they draw out and explore different aspects of the meaning of faith in the risen Christ: gift, surprise, conversion, forgiveness,[17] friendship and closeness, evangelising mission.[18] But they are based on the real experiences of the early disciples. Because of what God has done for his Son in raising him from death, new possibilities have been opened up for human beings; our understanding of God and our relationship with God have been changed.[19] For each of the stories I will seek to uncover the theological message(s), and then offer some reflections concerning what they may offer us for our spirituality, our Gospel living. With this background we can now pursue our examination of the narratives.

In presenting this book I acknowledge my enormous debt to the writings of numerous scholars that I have consulted over the years, which are summarised in these pages, and to which I make frequent reference in the endnotes. Their learning, insights and integrity have been instructive and inspirational. I have tried to write in a non-technical style, hoping that this book will be accessible to a wide readership, lay, religious and clergy of all denominations, who wish to deepen their understanding of the resurrection of Jesus and its meaning, and to explore the implications of discipleship for today. The endnotes provide additional useful information but are by no means an essential read. The text can be used for personal study, prayer and reflection, and also for Christian groups of various kinds: prayer groups, bible study groups, RCIA groups, and also for retreatants, teachers, catechists and students at different levels.

I have dedicated this book to Fr Francis J. Moloney, SDB, AM, D.Phil (Oxon), FAHA. Frank has been a great friend and support for over fifty years since we first met at the Salesian University in Rome. I am deeply indebted to him also for the inspiration of his scholarship, especially in deepening my appreciation and understanding of the Gospels of Mark and John. I am very grateful to Revd. Canon Prof. Dorothy A. Lee, FAHA, for kindly agreeing to write a foreword to this book, to Fr Kieran Anderson, SDB, for proofreading the text and making

6

helpful and constructive comments, and to Dr John Lydon, KCHS, FHEA, for reading the manuscript and offering an appreciation for the back cover. I thank Fr Bob Gardner, SDB, and the staff of Don Bosco Publications, Sarah Seddon and Bernadette Gaskell, for their patience, care and expertise in preparing the manuscript for publication.

Finally, I thank my Salesian confrères and many other friends, contemporary disciples of Jesus, for their encouragement, inspiration and support over the years. It is my hope and wish that this book may help many readers to come to know more deeply our risen Lord, and to proclaim his aliveness particularly through their/our own aliveness.

Michael T. Winstanley, SDB.
Thornleigh House, Bolton.
Oct 1, 2018.

Notes

1   Though without the sadness of Horace (Odes **II**, 14): "*Eheu, fugaces labuntur anni.*" ("Alas, the fleeting years glide swiftly by").

2   James D.G. Dunn, *Jesus Remembered* (Cambridge: Eerdmans, 2003), 826, states that belief in the resurrection "seems to have been not only fundamental for Christianity as far back as we can trace, but also presuppositional and foundational." José A. Pagola, *Jesus: An Historical Approximation* (Miami: Convivium Press, 2011), 393, maintains that "For believers in Jesus it is the most real, important and decisive event that has ever occurred in human history, because it is the foundation and true hope of history." For Charles H. Dodd, *The Founder of Christianity* (London: Collins, 1971), 169, the resurrection is the belief around which the church itself grew up, and the 'given' upon which its faith was based.

3   Francis J. Moloney, *The Resurrection of the Messiah* (New York: Paulist Press, 2013), 128, prefers this date.

4   For what follows see Raymond E. Brown, *The Virginal Conception and Bodily Resurrection of Jesus* (London: Chapmans, 1974), 78–80; Beda Rigaux, *Dio l'ha risuscitato,* (Milan: Edizioni Paoline, 1976), 160–166, 209–232; Pagola, *Jesus,* 388–390.

5   Dunn, *Jesus Remembered,* 826, n. 4; it is presupposed again and again in the earliest Christian writings.

6   Brown, *Bodily Resurrection,* 79, points out that in some twenty passages it is stated that the Father raised Jesus. In fact, Rowan Williams, *God with Us,* (London: SPCK, 2017), 67–68, maintains that the fact that God has raised Jesus now becomes God's identifying characteristic; God comes to be defined in relation to Jesus and his resurrection.

7   Brown, *Bodily Resurrection,* 74–75. Gerald O'Collins, *The Easter Jesus* (London: DLT, 1973), 50–53, maintains that originally 'resurrection' and 'exaltation' were relatively independent interpretations of the same event; the theme of 'exaltation' emerges as a comment on and subsequent interpretation of the resurrection. Dunn, *Jesus Remembered,* 868, believes that exaltation would have been the most obvious category for those who saw 'Jesus alive from the dead' to use as they attempted to articulate or make sense (it amounts to the same thing) of what they saw. The thought of exaltation is combined with (rather than understood as an alternative to) the pre-dominant category of resurrection. As Brown, *Bodily Resurrection,* 74, says, 'exaltation' language need have done no more than capture the eschatological aspect of the resurrection. For Pagola, *Jesus,* 389, the two terms enrich and complement each other.

8   Brown, *Bodily Resurrection,* 76. Christopher F. Evans, *Resurrection and the New Testament,* (London: SCM Press, 1970), 132, writes that the central place of resurrection faith in the New Testament could not be explained or expected either from contemporary Judaism or from the preaching of Jesus. Gerald O'Collins, *Easter Faith: Believing in the Risen Jesus* (London: DLT, 2003), 41–42, observes that there were many beliefs about the existence or non-existence of life after death in the Jewish and pagan worlds, but nothing closely resembling what the first Christians were proclaiming about Jesus. In *Easter Jesus,* 47, he notes that belief in the resurrection emerged late in the history of Israel (Daniel and 2 Maccabees); also Pagola, *Jesus,* 395–96. N. Tom Wright, *The Resurrection of the Son of God* (London: SPCK, 2003), 206, concludes: "The world of Judaism had generated from its rich scriptural origins, a rich variety of beliefs about what happened, and would happen to the dead. But it was quite unprepared for the new mutation which sprang up, like a totally unexpected plant, within the already well-stocked garden." See also Gerhard Lohfink, *Is This All There Is? On Resurrection and Eternal Life* (Collegeville, MN: Liturgical Press, 2017), 57–93; and *Jesus of Nazareth: What He Wanted, Who He Was* (Collegeville, MN: Liturgical Press, 2012), 295–96, where he refers to exaltation, rapture or translation and general resurrection; Sandra Schneiders, 'The Resurrection (of the Body) in the Fourth Gospel: A Key to Johannine Spirituality', in John R. Donahue, (ed.), *Life in Abundance: Studies in John's Gospel in Tribute to Raymond E. Brown* (Collegeville, MN: Liturgical Press, 2005), 173–176. Dunn, *Jesus Remembered,* 866–870, notes other ways available to affirm Jesus' vindication: translation or rapture (as Enoch or Elijah (Gen 5:24; 2 Kgs 2:11–12), though this excluded death;

vindication/exaltation (Wis 3:1–9; 5:1–5; Dan 7). Resurrection hope in Jesus' day was in terms of general or final resurrection prior to final judgement.

9   See Brown, *Bodily Resurrection*, 81–96; Reginald H. Fuller, *The Formation of the Resurrection Narratives* (London: SPCK, 1972), 9–35; Wright, *Resurrection*, 312–360; Rigaux, *Dio l'ha risuscitato*, 173–191; Evans, *Resurrection*, 41–56; O'Collins, *The Easter Jesus*, 3–17.

10   O'Collins, *Easter Jesus*, 4. The language of the first section is not Pauline (e.g. Paul prefers "sin" in the singular; nowhere else does he refer to the "twelve"). He could have learnt the formula in Antioch; it may have originated in Jerusalem. The fact of the appearances is stated; there is no attempt at a description of what happened. Lohfink, *Jesus of Nazareth*, 291, believes the ancient creed probably ended with the Twelve.

11   Brown, *Bodily Resurrection*, 124, notes that the reference to "the third day" in the formula probably derives from the discovery of the empty tomb, since Christians did not attempt to date the eschatological event of resurrection itself. It is possible that the phrase in Paul "implies the discovery of the empty tomb and the interpretation of that event by a faith engendered by the post-resurrection appearances."

12   Pope Benedict XVI, *Jesus of Nazareth*, (San Francisco: Ignatius Press, 2011), 2:248, distinguishes the confessional tradition and the narrative tradition.

13   Wright, *Resurrection*, 660, affirms that the individual evangelists have clearly felt free to shape and retell their stories in such a way as to bring out their own particular emphases and theological intentions. Williams, *God with Us*, 76, describes the resurrection stories as "abrupt, confused, vivid and unpolished"; their untidiness is one of the main reasons for taking them seriously as historical reportage. He notes the lack of Old Testament echoes. The Gospel accounts are pressed into existence by facts; they do not fit into any pre-existing pattern. Nothing like it had happened previously; it is an event which inaugurates something completely new (pp. 77–80).

14   O'Collins, *The Easter Jesus*, 23, 36–38, notes that in Paul's list of recipients of resurrection appearances (1 Cor 15:3–8), he provides no geographical details. The important thing is that Jesus was raised and appeared; *where* Jesus met his disciples matters little. Peter and the disciples are the primary witnesses to the resurrection: that is the historical truth, wherever the evangelists place them.

15   Wright, *Resurrection*, 587. See Moloney, *Resurrection*, 137.

16   As Sandra Schneiders "The Resurrection (of the Body) in the Fourth Gospel", 170, puts it: the text as it stands gives us access to new possibilities of Christian living in the world.

17   Pagola, *Jesus*, 400, comments that Schillebeeckx sees forgiveness as the matrix in which faith in Jesus as the risen one is born. Williams, *Resurrection* (3rd

edition), (London: DLT, 2014), xii, sees the resurrection stories as having to do with a sense of the absolution by God, creating forgiven persons, whose relation with God, and, derivatively with each other, is transformed.

18   Pagola, *Jesus*, 392, 399. The stories do have a basis in reality. They recall experiences of Jesus' unexpected presence; early uncertainties and doubts; a process of conversion; reflection on scripture; a sense of mission.

19   Moloney, *Resurrection*, 148, concludes: "There is no 'knock-down' objective historical proof for the resurrection events reported in the Gospel narratives. But there is objective evidence that the earliest Church came into existence because of the encounter with the risen Jesus—whatever that means." He quotes Sanders: "That Jesus' followers (and later Paul) had resurrection experiences is, in my judgement, a fact. What the reality was that gave rise to the experiences I do not know."

Chapter One
The Resurrection in Mark

Traditions concerning the life, death and resurrection of Jesus circulated in oral form among the Christian communities for many years before Mark brought a selection together in the form of a narrative, the Gospel we know.[1] His compilation, which proclaims his deep faith, exhibits considerable theological acumen and literary skill. It has been referred to as a passion narrative with a long introduction.[2] Certainly his presentation of the passion and death of Jesus is a powerful piece of writing. One of its main theological themes is the aloneness of Jesus, as he is betrayed by one of his closest followers, abandoned by all the others in the garden of arrest and later denied with a curse by his main disciple. The religious leaders of his nation unanimously find him guilty, the Jerusalem populace opt for the release of Barabbas, the murderer, rather than Jesus, and shout that he should be handed over to the hideous torture death of crucifixion. On the cross he is mocked by people, soldiery and scribes, and even the two thieves disown him. There is no mother or beloved disciple on Calvary, and the women who are present stand at a distance. The searing anguish of his pain and loneliness and failure is focused and captured in the loud cry from the cross: "My God, my God, why hast thou forsaken me?" He dies utterly alone.[3]

After the death of the Baptist in Herod's prison, his disciples came, took away his body and buried it in a tomb.[4] In the case of Jesus this service is performed by a stranger, a non-Galilean Sanhedrin member, a pious, observant Jew "waiting expectantly for the kingdom of God," the fulfilment of God's promises.[5] Since the Law required that a criminal's corpse should not be left to hang on the cross after sunset, especially if the next day was a Sabbath,[6] his request is an expression of his desire to fulfil God's Will and is an act of piety. In Jesus' time the burial of corpses was taken very seriously and was seen as a necessary good which overshadowed any ritual impurity.[7] Jesus' unusually quick death is a surprise for Pilate,[8] perhaps arousing some suspicion, so he verifies the facts with the centurion. The death of Jesus is confirmed by the centurion, which leaves Pilate free to grant Joseph's request and allow the corpse to be handed over. The burial is hurried; there is no mention of washing or anointing the body, nor is there any indication of the customary lamentation. The women followers of Jesus do not get involved. The burial of Jesus is, technically, a dishonourable burial.[9] The women simply observe; they are witnesses to what is happening.[10] They know the location of the grave. They will be key players in the next phase of the drama.

The distress, darkness and horror of the story of Jesus' passion and death are lightened, however, by the rich symbolism of the tearing of the temple veil, and by the climactic comment of the centurion: "Truly this man was God's Son" (15:39). These are powerful hints that the vindication hoped for by Jesus will be realised. Mark proclaims this vindication in his narrative of the Empty Tomb.[11] The theme of the failure of the disciples is also taken up again, as the ever-faithful Jesus invites the women to instruct them to meet him once more in Galilee. The original Gospel then ends rather abruptly at 16:8, without any account of Jesus' appearances or sayings.[12] According to the vast majority of scholars, the remaining verses, alternative endings found in some manuscripts, were added later by scribes in order to fill the gap.[13]

The text concerning the tomb reads:

> When the sabbath was over, Mary Magdalene, and Mary the mother of James, and Salome bought spices, so that they might go and anoint him. And very early on the first day of the week, when the sun had risen, they went to the tomb. They had been saying to one another, "Who will roll away the stone for us from the entrance to the tomb?" When they looked up, they saw that the stone, which was very large, had already been rolled back. As they entered the tomb, they saw a young man, dressed in a white robe, sitting on the right side; and they were alarmed. But he said to them, "Do not be alarmed; you are looking for Jesus of Nazareth, who was crucified. He has been raised; he is not here. Look, there is the place they laid him. But go, tell his disciples and Peter that he is going ahead of you to Galilee; there you will see him, just as he told you." So they went out and fled from the tomb, for terror and amazement had seized them; and they said nothing to anyone, for they were afraid. (16:1–8)

The Setting (1–4)

With his introductory phrase "When the Sabbath was over", Mark resumes his narrative after the silence of the Sabbath rest and links the Easter story with his description of the death and the subsequent burial of Jesus.[14] The women are named as Mary Magdalene, Mary the mother of James, and Salome. They were present on Calvary, "looking on from a distance".[15] Not having obtained spices on Friday, and having observed the Sabbath faithfully, the women go on Saturday evening to buy some, presumably with a view to using them next morning. Early on that Sunday morning, "the first day of the week",[16] after the rising of the sun,[17] they make the journey to the tomb in which Jesus was buried. Its location they know because of their presence at the burial. Because of the hurried nature of Jesus' burial, and also because it was 'dishonourable', their intention seems to be to rectify the omission.[18] Presumably, they were also motivated by grief and loving devotion; perhaps they also sought some sort of closure.[19] As readers we recall the anointing of Jesus in Simon's house at Bethany, which he interpreted in terms of an anticipation of his burial: "she has anointed my body beforehand for its burial" (14:8). It was not unusual in that culture for relatives to visit the grave for three days after burial; in fact, mourning was at its height on the third day. Perhaps it was unrealistic of the women in such a climate to think of anointing a corpse after three days but love and concern often override practical considerations.[20] From their actions it is clear that they are concerned about a corpse; the possibility of Jesus' resurrection has never entered their heads.

While on the way, the women wonder how they will manage to roll the stone away from the tomb entrance, given its size. As a good storyteller, Mark is creating dramatic tension and excitement, preparing for the amazing and totally unexpected surprise which follows. For, on arriving, they find the tomb open, the large stone already rolled away.[21] The passive verb indicates the action of God; the women look up and "see" what God has done.[22]

The Easter Proclamation (5–7)

Having moved inside the tomb, the women find "a young man" in a white robe, the traditional attire of heavenly beings; he is seated on the right-hand side, the position of an authoritative teacher.[23] This figure is presumably an interpreting angel.[24] The women are overcome with amazement and fear at this unexpected occurrence; the verb indicates intense feelings of awe at the numinous, the reaction which normally accompanies heavenly manifestations.[25] After seeking to dispel the women's fear, the role of the angelic youth is to proclaim the Easter message:

> Do not be alarmed; you are looking for Jesus of Nazareth, who was crucified. He has been raised; he is not here. Look, there is the place they laid him.

The death of Jesus is not the end of his story. "He has been raised, he is not here". His faithful God and Father has not forsaken him, but has vindicated him, as Jesus had foretold, dramatically reversing his apparent failure, and conquering death. Jesus is named as "Jesus of Nazareth" (the "Nazarene", *ton Nazarēnon*), as at the outset of Mark's narrative.[26] In this way the evangelist draws together his entire story, and indicates that "the Jesus whom God has raised from the dead is no other Jesus than the one with whom he began his story, namely the Jesus who is God's beloved Son."[27] The startling antithesis and contrast between "was crucified", and "was raised" by God is typical of the kerygmatic formulas and faith confessions of the early church, as we have seen.[28] The insight of the centurion into the true identity of Jesus is confirmed. The formula rings out like a triumphant shout of victory. Through the angel/young man, God proclaims the resurrection of the Son. "Human experience and expectation have been transcended by the action of God."[29] After the proclamation comes a reference to the tomb, the place where "they" had laid him, and now the reason for its emptiness becomes evident.

But Jesus' death is not the end of the story for the disciples either. The messenger continues:

> But go and give this message to his disciples and Peter: "He is going on before you into Galilee; there you will see him, as he told you."

The women are sent on mission to the disciples, leaving the empty tomb behind. In spite of their failure and flight, their choice not to "be with" him, their unwillingness to accept the shame of belonging to him, they are still considered to be his disciples.[30] In spite of his threefold denial, his emphatically sworn choice no longer to "be with" Jesus, Peter is still singled out for special mention.[31] The risen Lord remains faithful; he has forgiven them, and he calls them back to him once more in Galilee, as promised (14:28), where it had all begun, where they had been with him, been taught by him, witnessed his mighty deeds and had experienced mission. On the way from the supper room to Gethsemane, as in the prophet Zechariah's words, Jesus foretold his death and the fact that they would be scattered, he had also promised that he would go before them shepherd-like to Galilee.[32] The words are here repeated, with the additional assurance that they will "see" him there.[33] If the disciples respond to the message by following Jesus to Galilee, they will see him, see him with new eyes, come to genuine faith and clearer understanding.[34] The scattered sheep will be gathered again, the journey of discipleship will begin anew, mission will be undertaken, especially to the Gentiles (see 13:10).[35]

The Sequel v. 8

The final verse of Mark's Gospel narrative is something of a puzzle:

> So they went out and fled from the tomb, for terror and amazement had seized them; and they said nothing to anyone, for they were afraid.

The women, who had remained true and stood by Jesus when all the men failed, are now overcome by fear and astonishment, terror and consternation, and they, too, take flight. Their fear is connected with the appearance and message of the "young man". In the face of God's action, a reaction of fear is not unnatural and is a common biblical feature. They are unable to cope with the experience and the news.

Their ongoing silence, expressed in a double negative, is, however, more problematic. Many scholarly explanations have been put forward. A frequently adduced view is that perhaps Mark is seeking to underline the mystery, wonder, awesomeness and supernatural character of resurrection.[36] Perhaps he wishes to emphasise our human inadequacy in the face of God's action. Maybe he wanted God to have the last word, the God who bestows the gift of Easter faith.[37] "Throughout the gospel men and women have been blind and deaf to the truth about Jesus, and now at the end, when the divine message is delivered to the women, they are struck dumb, and fail to deliver it."[38] It is Mark's final irony. Frequently, Jesus has told folk to say nothing about the truth they have glimpsed, and they have disobeyed. Now that their time has come to report what has happened, the women are silent! Even the women fail; "their disobedience and fear demonstrate their inability to believe the good news."[39] The verse with which the Gospel ends "drives home with considerable force the women's sharing in one of the fundamental aspects of the disciples' failure to follow Jesus to the cross: fear (4:41; 6:50; 9:32; 10:32)."[40] The women join the other disciples in their failure.

It is clear from the other Gospels and from Paul that the early Christian communities were aware of the appearances of the risen Jesus. Their faith was founded on this. Mark seems to have changed the story. The reader will presume that, like his other predictions and promises, this promise of Jesus, reiterated by the "young man" at the tomb, will also come true. The Christian reader knows that it did, otherwise there would be no Gospel and no believing and celebrating Christian community. Mark takes all initiative away from human beings, for they all fail; he places it with the overspilling goodness, incredible faithfulness and gratuitous love of God.[41] It is the Father's transforming action that has vindicated the Son's generous and loving self-gift in death. And it is the Father's action that has transformed the fearful and failed disciples and brought the Christian community into existence. Mark proclaims and articulates the faith of this community in the opening verse and prologue of his Gospel (1:1–13). His story challenges us, centuries later, to accept Jesus' way, and in our struggles and failures assures us of God's ongoing faithfulness, trustworthiness and transforming power. By ending as he does, the masterstroke of a storyteller,[42] Mark "leaves his readers, who may have thought that the story was about somebody else, with a decision to make ..."[43] The end of the Gospel, like the prologue (1:1–13), addresses the reader. "The promise of the Gospel's prologue (1:1–13) is fulfilled in the action of God described in its epilogue (16:1–8) and experienced by believing readers of the Markan story."[44]

Reflections

In some ways, the ending of Mark's Gospel is bleak. Both women and men fail; they are indeed "fallible followers", to use Malbon's terminology.[45] We admit that we probably find ourselves in their company. Failure and fear are part of our experience, too, centuries later. In fact, the number of times that key figures in the Bible are instructed by God not to be afraid illustrates the pervasive nature of fear. No other command or exhortation is more frequently made. Fear can hold us back from surrendering to God and God's involving us in His saving plan. Perhaps it is the fear of losing ourselves, of losing control over our lives; maybe it is the fear of being found wanting, of being inadequate. Fear can often prevent us from reaching out to others; it can be an obstacle to friendship and intimacy, to community and collaboration, to service and self-giving; fear can make it extremely difficult to trust others. Fear can stifle compassion, thwart growth, deaden dreams, cramp initiative, crush potential, sap life energy. Fear can severely hinder genuine discernment. So much of the violence and aggression within us and around us in our country and our wider world is born of fear and is sustained and fuelled by it. We can be afraid of challenge, of failure, of being marginalised, of becoming useless. We can be afraid of what others may think or say. We can be afraid of suffering and of death.

We can, however, take heart, for the God behind Mark's story and our story is always faithful. And the Jesus He calls his "Son, the Beloved", is faithful too. Throughout the breathless narrative subsequent to his lakeside encounter with the two pairs of fishermen, Jesus has remained true to his disciples, despite their fragility, dullness and capacity to get it wrong, spectacularly at times. Beyond the tragic mess and failure of that final week in Jerusalem, he summons them back to Galilee to start again. In the Old Testament, God is understood above all as faithful love. This is the God made known in Jesus. This is how the darkness of Calvary is transformed into the bright dawn of Easter day. This is how our own shadows and darkness and fears, too, will be transformed, as God's faithful love is revealed in our own life experience as fallible disciples of Jesus.

Notes

1   Mark probably wrote soon after 70 CE, the year of the destruction of Jerusalem by the Romans. A long tradition maintains that he wrote in Rome, and a majority of scholars still accept this view. Others suggest a place closer to Palestine, like southern Syria. Most commentaries on Mark deal with these issues in some detail. The text of this chapter is a revision of material to be found in my *Jesus and the Little People* (Bolton: Don Bosco Publications, 2012), 163–171.

2   Mark 1:1–15 is sometimes referred to as the prologue to the Gospel, and 16:1–8 as the epilogue. M. Eugene Boring, *Mark. A Commentary* (NTL Louisville & London: Westminster John Knox, 2006), 441, notes that epilogue does not mean appendix or optional supplement. "As the prologue gives the prospective framework within which the narrative as a whole is to be understood, so the epilogue provides the retrospective key to the whole."

3   See Michael T. Winstanley, *Come and See* (London: DLT, 1985), 100-110; Lohfink, *Jesus of Nazareth*, 289.

4   6:29.

5   See Francis J. Moloney, *The Gospel of Mark. A Commentary* (Peabody,

MA: Hendrickson, 2002), 333; Dennis E. Nineham, *St. Mark* (London: Penguin
Books, 1963), 434; Morna D. Hooker, *The Gospel according to St.
Mark* (London: A&C Black, 1991), 381; George Martin, *The Gospel according to Mark* (Chicago:
Loyola, 2005), 444; Raymond E. Brown, *The Death of the Messiah*, 2 vols (London:
Chapmans, 1994), 2:1216. The phrase can apply to pious observers of the Law. Earlier
(14:34) the good scribe is described as being "not far from the kingdom of God".
John R. Donahue & Donald H. Harrington, *The Gospel of Mark* (Collegeville, MN:
Liturgical Press, 2002), 456, link him with this scribe in being examples of the best
in the religious tradition of Israel. For Luke, Joseph is "a good and righteous man,"
a Sanhedrin member "who had not agreed with their plan and action". N. Tom
Wright, *Mark for Everyone* (London: SPCK, 2001), 220, maintains that he must
have been a secret supporter of Jesus, which is the view of John 19:38. For Matthew
(27:57) he is "a disciple of Jesus". Perhaps he was a later convert (Brendan Byrne, *A
Costly Freedom* (Collegeville, MN: Liturgical Press, 2008), 259). In favour of a burial
of Jesus by the Jews, see Acts 13:27–29; John 19:31; Pet 6:21.

6   Deut 21:22–23. The Jews usually buried the dead on the day of death if
possible, though not on the Sabbath.

7   Brown, *Death,* **2,** 1216; Martin, *Mark,* 445.

8   Pilate also "wondered" at the silence of Jesus (15:5).

9   Brown, *Death,* **2,** 1243–44.

10   Brown, *Death,* **2,** 1218; R. A. Culpepper, *Mark* (Macon, GA: Smyth &
Helwys, 2007), 571; Martin, *Mark,* 447. Byrne, *Costly Freedom,* 249, suggests that
they fulfil the function of the two or more witnesses required by the Law (Deut
19:15). Donahue and Harrington, *Mark,* 455, note that the imperfect tense of the
verb suggests the women "took in everything from start to finish."

11   Resurrection *faith* existed long before Mark, as we have seen in the
Introduction; scholars hold differing views as to what extent Mark's *account* is based
on pre-Markan tradition. (See Boring, *Mark,* 443; Moloney, *Gospel,* 342, n. 13).

12   Boring, *Mark,* 442, comments that Mark is concerned to affirm the reality
of the resurrection, but not to narrate it in a way that requires fitting it into a
conceptual and chronological framework.

13   Some scholars have thought that Mark's original ending was lost, the final
section of the scroll being worn away or detached; others that he was prevented by
sickness or death from continuing as he had intended. But most now feel it best
to assume that he ended where he wanted to end, in spite of the bad Greek! See
Byrne, *Costly Freedom,* 253; Nineham, *Mark,* 439–442; Donald Senior, *The Passion
of Jesus in the Gospel of Mark* (Wilmington, DE: Glazier, 1984), 135; Dunn, *Jesus
Remembered,* 826, n. 7, who refers to "a very broad consensus". Moloney, *Gospel,*
339–341, discusses this in detail, concluding that the original Gospel ended at 16:8.
N. Tom Wright, *Resurrection,* 616–624, however, argues strongly that Mark did

continue beyond 16:8, so that Jesus' prophetic words would be fulfilled; Matthew probably filled out his schematic form. Moloney, *Resurrection*, 5–6, addresses the additional endings found in the NRSV (the shorter ending and the longer, 9–10 and 9–20); scribes provided alternative endings more in conformity with the endings of the other Gospels. None of the endings can claim authenticity. Sandra M. Schneiders, *Jesus Risen in our Midst: Essays on the Resurrection of Jesus in the Fourth Gospel*, (Collegeville, MN: Liturgical Press, 2013), 12, observes that this section of Mark is probably a conflation of stories from the other Gospels, but it does offer corroboration of the most important narratives of Easter appearances. Dunn, *Jesus Remembered*, 826, n.7, opines that the longer ending shows knowledge of Luke, John and Acts; it was probably added to Mark 16 to round off the Gospel more satisfactorily in the second century. Brown, *Bodily Resurrection*, 98, believes that Mark ended at 16:8; he also believes that the writer of the Appendix may have drawn on sources similar to the canonical Gospels rather than on the Gospels themselves.

14   It is therefore "the third day" (8:31; 9:31; 10:34; 14:58; 15:29).

15   On Calvary (15:40) the second Mary is said to be the mother of James the younger and Joses; these women "used to follow him and provided for him when he was in Galilee". At the burial (15:47), there is no mention of Salome, and the Mary is named as the mother (or daughter) of Joses. Mark makes no attempt to harmonise his lists. Hooker, *Mark*, 383, suggests that he was probably reproducing different independent traditions; similarly, Culpepper, *Mark*, 584.

16   Boring, *Mark*, 443, notes that the reference to "the first day of the week" reflects early Christian practice of meeting together on the Lord's Day (1 Cor 16:2; Acts 20:7).

17   Byrne, *Costly Freedom*, 254, calls this a highly evocative allusion, a dawn ripe with promise of renewed creation. In a similar vein Moloney, *Gospel*, 343, sees light now dawning as God enters the story. Mark's two time references are not consistent; he often uses duplicate time expressions, the second more precise than the first. Donahue and Harrington, *Mark*, 457, suggest the two references are best taken as referring to the same thing; that is, about 6 am. Culpepper, *Mark*, 585, points out that Mark often uses double references, and sometimes awkwardly. He also notes the view that they set out in the dark, but that it was light when they arrived; Moloney, *Gospel*, 343, n. 19, would see this view as "probably correct".

18   This is Luke's view also; in John, since Jesus received a lavish burial as befits a king, the purpose for Magdalene's visit was simply to mourn.

19   Boring, *Mark*, 443.

20   But, as Nineham, *Mark*, 443, remarks, those who collected and handed on the traditions were presumably well aware of local customs, attitudes and conditions. See also Brown, *Risen Christ*, 12, n. 9, who suggests that Mark is a better guide to plausibility in burial practices than a 20th-century scholar with limited available

20

knowledge about burial in that period. The bringing of spices to anoint the body is omitted in Matthew (28:1) and Luke (24:1), though Luke does contain a reference to spices. (See Moloney, *Resurrection,* 8). The purpose of the anointing was to reduce the odour of decomposition.

21   Fuller, *The Formation of the Resurrection Narratives,* 54, and Brown, *Bodily Resurrection,* 121, n. 203, maintain that this detail of the rolled back stone may be very ancient, and belong to the earliest form of the tradition. The perfect tense of the passive verb suggests that the effect of the rolling away of the stone would last forever. As Culpepper, *Mark,* 585, points out, the emphasis on the size of the stone highlights the wonder of God's action. Moloney, *Resurrection,* 9, notes that it is the God "to whom Jesus cried out in anguish in his dying moments (15:34)" who has intervened. Boring, *Mark,* 443–44 notes that the narrative is not concerned with logic or psychology; the comment about the stone is for the benefit of the reader; it emphasises that the women have no expectation of finding it removed and the tomb empty. The statement stands in the same series as God's hand splitting the heavens (1:10) and rending the temple curtain (15:38). "The resurrection will be the divine finale of removing barriers that separate God and the world."

22   The text contains two verbs: "when they looked up, they saw the stone". Moloney, *Resurrection,* 9, comments that this heightens the solemnity of the moment; it is no ordinary seeing. Boring, *Mark,* 444, links this verb (*anablépein*) with its use in 8:24, where it is used for the preliminary and partial healing of the blind man of Bethsaida. The women resemble him; unlike Bartimaeus (10:52), they do not attain full sight within Mark's narrative.

23   Boring, *Mark,* 445. The reference to the "young man" (*neaniskos*), which recalls the "young man" of the arrest scene who fled away naked (14:51–52), may be a hint of God's power to reverse also the failure of the disciples. See Moloney, *Gospel,* 345–46; *Resurrection,* 10–11. Culpepper, *Mark,* 586–87, is open to the symbolism, but considers it as secondary. Not all scholars agree with this connection. Angels are represented as young men in 2 Macc 3:26, 33; 5:2. Dunn, *Jesus Remembered,* 829, n.12, maintains that almost certainly Mark intended the "young man" to be understood as an angel. It was quite typical in the Old Testament to describe an appearing angel as a young man and describe heavenly beings as clothed in white.

24   Matt 28:2 and Luke 24:23 interpret it this way. The interpreting angel is a feature of apocalyptic literature (see Zech 1–6; Dan 7–12; Rev 1:1; 19:9-22:16). See Moloney, *Gospel,* 345; Wilfrid Harrington, *Mark* (Dublin: Veritas, 1979), 244; Denis McBride, *The Gospel of Mark* (Dublin: Dominican Publications, 1996), 262; Culpepper, *Mark,* 586; Brown, *Death,* 1, 299–300. The simplest account of the Empty Tomb is that reflected in John (see ch.4, John 20). The emptiness of the tomb did not give rise to resurrection faith. It was the appearances of Jesus to his disciples which gave rise to faith, as well as providing the explanation why the tomb was empty. In passing on the tradition, it was necessary to insert an explanation. An accepted literary manner of doing so was to put the message on the lips of an angel. Then the

Empty Tomb narrative becomes the vehicle for the proclamation of Easter faith: "he has been raised". This is the text which we are now considering. See Brown, *Bodily Resurrection*, 123.

25   See 9:15; 14:33.

26   Brown, *Risen Christ*, 1–14, sees this as an inclusion with 1:25–27, where the demon addresses Jesus as "Jesus the Nazarene". "This makes the reader certain that the same person who at the beginning of the Gospel manifested his power over evil is the one in whom God now manifests His power over death."

27   Jack Dean Kingsbury, *The Christology of Mark's Gospel* (Philadelphia: Fortress, 1983), 153; Brown, *Risen Christ*, 13–14. See 1:23; 10:47; 14:67. As Culpepper states, *Mark*, 587, the angel's words are a summary of the early Christian preaching. On p. 588 he notes that "the Nazarene" was the descendant of David who would build the temple.

28   The perfect tense (*estaurōmenon*) is used here, indicating a past event which continues: Jesus' identity remains the "crucified one". Boring, *Mark*, 441, n. b, comments that "the crucifixion is not an episode in the past that is left behind at the resurrection. Even after the resurrection, Jesus' identity continues as the Crucified One." The second verb (*ēgerthē*) is aorist tense (past definite), as in Rom 6:4; 7:4; 8:34; 2 Cor 5:15. It expresses a decisive action which has occurred, the act of passing from death to life; it is the divine passive, indicating the action of God. Paul uses the term "crucified" rather than "died" in 1 Cor 1:23; 2:2; Gal 3:1; 5:24; it is found also in Acts 2:36; 4:10.

29   Moloney, *Resurrection*, 11.

30   In 3:13–15, discipleship is defined as to "be with" Jesus and to "be sent".

31   Boring, *Mark*, 442, n. c, suggests that *kai* can be understood here either as "especially" or "even." Even Peter can be restored. Harrington, *Mark*, 245, also.

32   14:27–28; in that verse the verb "see" is not used, though it is perhaps implied, (Byrne, *Costly Freedom*, 256), and the verb is future tense.

33   Probably this time the verb (*proagein*), here in the present tense, means that Jesus is preceding them, will get there first.

34   Boring, *Mark*, 446, suggests that Jesus is still "on the way", as in the ministry.

35   For Boring, *Mark*, 447, Galilee "represents the openness to Jesus' message of the later Gentile church." The future of the people of God is no longer bound up with Jerusalem and its temple.

36   Nineham, *Mark*, 448. Moloney, *Gospel*, 349, calls this the traditional solution to the problem.

37   Hugh Anderson, *The Gospel of Mark* (London: Oliphants, 1976), 358.

Byrne, *Costly Freedom*, 258, suggests that Mark wishes to emphasise that resurrection faith was not the result of the empty tomb or the women's testimony, but because the disciples "saw" the Lord.

38   Hooker, *Mark*, 387; Martin, *Mark*, 452.

39   Hooker, *Mark*, 387. Elizabeth S. Malbon, *In the Company of Jesus: Characters in Mark's Gospel* (Louisville: Westminster John Knox, 2000), 204, observes that these three women are better designated as "fallible followers", like the male disciples.

40   Moloney, *Gospel*, 349; *Resurrection*, 13. Brown, *Risen Christ*, 16–17, suggests that some in Mark's community may have failed under persecution and could find encouragement in the failure of the male disciples. Others may not yet have been tested; like the women they may fail if they are overcome with fear. Discipleship involves suffering. "The resurrection cannot be appropriated unless one has been tried." Culpepper, *Mark*, 589, comments that the theme of human failure is complete; the religious authorities, Jesus' hometown, the disciples, the crowds, the Roman authorities and even the women who accompanied him to Jerusalem failed him. Wright, *Mark*, 221–224, argues that Mark probably did write a conclusion in which the women told the disciples and Jesus appeared to them and gave them a commission. As it stands, however, we are invited to fill in the blank. See Culpepper, *Mark*, 589–90, for the arguments for and against. Dunn, *Jesus Remembered*, 830, n. 14, suggests that the effect is to relativise the role of the women and reinforce that of the disciples as primary witnesses of and for the resurrection. On p.832, n. 26, he notes that Mark clearly did not intend to suggest that the story died with the women. It got out and Mark knows it! "It is part of Mark's genius that he leaves his story open at the end, open for the congregations who hear it being read to carry it on from what they know happened thereafter and what they know from personal experience is still happening."

41   Moloney, *Gospel*, 348–354. There is something very Pauline in what Mark is attempting to do; Paul holds that God has saved us by his free gift of grace, available through the death and resurrection of Jesus. (See also ' "He is going before you into Galilee". Mark 16:6–8 and the Christian Community' in *Gospel Interpretation and Christian Life*, (Adelaide: ATF Press, 2017), 128, n. 22.

42   Moloney, *Resurrection*, 15.

43   Boring, 449. On 448, n. 14, he refers to the views of Focant, that the narrative circles back on itself as a spiral; the reader can now go back to the beginning with eyes to see and ears to hear. The epilogue of the Evangelist constitutes a prologue to the work of the reader. Dunn, *Jesus Remembered*, 832–833, n. 26, similarly: It is part of Mark's genius that he leaves his story open at the end, open for the congregations who hear it being read to carry it on from what they know happened thereafter and what they know from personal experience is still happening. Pagola, *Jesus*, 416–17, suggests that as readers we are invited to return to the

beginning of the story, and from the perspective of the resurrection, reflect on it anew, and come to 'see' the real identity of Jesus and the profound content of his activity and message.

44   Moloney, *Gospel*, 352–53. The exalted Christological claims of the prologue have been vindicated by the story of the suffering and crucified Jesus, especially by the Easter proclamation of the epilogue (16:1–8).

45   Malbon, *In the Company of Jesus*, 62–67.

Chapter Two
The Resurrection in Matthew

Matthew's presentation of the Easter events is more complex than that of Mark.[1] The story of the finding of the empty tomb is flanked by brief episodes recorded only in Matthew, episodes in which the religious authorities and a group of soldiers are involved: the first concerns the setting of guards at the tomb; the second, their report to the authorities. Obviously, these take place in a Jerusalem setting.[2] The women who make the journey to the tomb experience not only the presence of an angel, but they also encounter the risen Jesus. The appearance of Jesus to the eleven disciples, however, occurs later in Galilee.[3]

Events Around the Tomb

The Setting of The Guard

> The next day, that is, after the day of Preparation, the chief priests and the Pharisees gathered before Pilate and said, "Sir, we remember what that impostor said while he was still alive, 'After three days I will rise again.' Therefore, command that the tomb be made secure until the third day; otherwise his disciples may go and steal him away, and tell the people, 'He has been raised from the dead', and the last deception would be worse than the first." Pilate said to them, "You have a guard of soldiers; go, make it as secure as you can." So they went with the guard and made the tomb secure by sealing the stone. (27:62–66)

In the evening of Jesus' death, Joseph of Arimathea comes forward and approaches Pilate to ask for Jesus' body. Pilate agrees, and Joseph attends to the burial. Matthew presents Joseph as a disciple of Jesus, and a man of means. Joseph wraps Jesus' body in a clean linen cloth, and buries it in his own tomb, newly hewn in the rock, rolling a great stone to the entrance. Mary Magdalene and the other Mary are present and observe all that takes place.

Next day, which would be the Sabbath, the religious leaders approach Pilate.[4] The Pharisees, who opposed Jesus continually during the ministry but had no role in the passion, now return and join forces with the chief priests, who, along with the elders of the people, were responsible for Jesus' death.[5] Continuing their rejection of Jesus, and referring to him with contempt as "that imposter", they inform Pilate of Jesus' earlier words "After three days I will rise again."[6] It is therefore imperative that the tomb be made secure until the third day, lest his disciples steal the body and tell the people that he has been raised from the dead. Mention of Jesus' promises to rise on the third day and of the announcing of this to the people heightens the reader's expectation and is not without its irony.[7] Pilate's response can be interpreted in two ways. First, Pilate is unwilling to be further involved by providing his own soldiers for this purpose and tells the religious leaders with a touch of cynicism to see to it themselves, since they have their own guard. Alternatively, Pilate makes Roman guards available.[8] So the leaders go along to the tomb along with the guard and officially seal the entrance stone.[9] However, "sealing the stone and setting the guard will be infantile precautions against the power that God is about to release."[10]

The Women at The Tomb

After the sabbath, as the first day of the week was dawning, Mary Magdalene and the other Mary went to see the tomb. And suddenly there was a great earthquake; for an angel of the Lord, descending from heaven, came and rolled back the stone and sat on it. His appearance was like lightning, and his clothing white as snow. For fear of him the guards shook and became like dead men. But the angel said to the women, "Do not be afraid; I know that you are looking for Jesus who was crucified. He is not here; for he has been raised, as he said. Come, see the place where he lay. Then go quickly and tell his disciples, 'He has been raised from the dead, and indeed he is going ahead of you to Galilee; there you will see him.' This is my message for you." So they left the tomb quickly with fear and great joy, and ran to tell his disciples. Suddenly Jesus met them and said, "Greetings!" And they came to him, took hold of his feet, and worshipped him. Then Jesus said to them, "Do not be afraid; go and tell my brothers to go to Galilee; there they will see me." (28:1–10)

None of the evangelists attempts to describe the moment of resurrection itself, for it is not something that can be described; but "Matthew edges toward it."[11] Matthew introduces his story with a time reference: "after the Sabbath … the first day of the week"; it is therefore the third day.[12] There is probably symbolism intended in the phrase about dawn, for a new period of history is starting. The two women who were present at the burial of Jesus, Mary Magdalene and the other Mary, are named. They are the main human players in the narrative. They go to see the tomb, and to mourn; there is no mention of anointing the body with spices (26:12).

Matthew describes what happens next in language with an apocalyptic flavour, in continuity with his earlier description of the death of Jesus (27:51). An earthquake again occurs (Hag 2:6; Zech 14:5).[13] Then "an angel of the Lord" comes down from heaven, rolls the stone away from the entrance to the tomb and triumphantly sits on it.[14] The angel's appearance is said to be like lightning, and his clothing white as snow (see 17:2; Dan 10:6–7). Traditionally, events like these were associated with the coming of the Lord at the end of the world and the breaking in of the Kingdom; but Matthew understands them here as an indication of the turning point of the ages. The end has been anticipated. God is intervening in the story and entering history definitively.[15] The guards fall to the ground, frozen with fear and shock.

The traditional story now continues; this is the heart of the episode. The angel addresses the women, bidding them not to be afraid. There has been no explicit indication of any fear, but it is the usual reaction to God's presence. He articulates his awareness that they are there at the tomb because they are looking for Jesus, the Jesus whom they know to have been crucified (and buried). He informs them that Jesus "is not here", because already "he has been raised." He reminds them that Jesus had earlier indicated that this would happen. This is the Easter kerygma.[16] The women are then invited to enter the tomb and see the place where he had been laid to rest, now vacant. At this point they are given a commission. They are to go quickly to the disciples who presumably are still in the city, and tell them two things.[17] First, they are to announce that Jesus has been raised; secondly, that he will go ahead of the disciples to Galilee, where they will see him.[18] The women then leave the tomb without delay to proclaim the message of Easter, the first human beings to do so. They set out in fear, as the response to a heavenly presence, and in great joy because of what they have seen and heard.[19]

While en route to inform the disciples, the women are met by Jesus, who greets them.[20] Though the verb is normal for an everyday greeting (*chairete*), it links in with the (Easter) joy with which they left the tomb. The women recognise him, go over to him,[21] take hold of his feet and worship him.[22] Like the angel he tells them not to be afraid,[23] and commands them to tell his disciples to go to Galilee, promising that they will see him there.[24] Whereas the angel referred to the disciples, Jesus refers to his "brothers", a remarkable indication of forgiveness and rehabilitation after their failure. Jesus remains faithful to them. In Luke the testimony of the women is rejected by the disciples. This is not the case in Matthew, for the disciples do go to Galilee and Jesus does encounter them there.

The Guards and The Authorities

> While they were going, some of the guard went into the city and told the chief priests everything that had happened. After the priests had assembled with the elders, they devised a plan to give a large sum of money to the soldiers, telling them, "You must say, 'His disciples came by night and stole him away while we were asleep.' If this comes to the governor's ears, we will satisfy him and keep you out of trouble." So they took the money and did as they were directed. And this story is still told among the Jews to this day. (28:11–15)

As the women set out to fulfil their commission by going to the disciples and announcing the remarkable news of the resurrection of Jesus, some members of the guard return to the chief priests in the city and report to them "everything that had happened." The chief priests are now the focus of attention. Clearly this disconcerting news about an empty tomb demands serious attention, and so a formal meeting takes place between priests and elders. They seem to accept the facts, but their hearts and mindset remain unchanged; there is not the slightest movement towards faith. To neutralise the consequences of what has occurred, they adopt the plan of bribing the soldiers, giving them a large amount of money, not unlike their Judas arrangement with silver coins in 26:14–16. They issue the order that they are to state that the disciples came during the night while they were asleep and took the body away. This attempt to explain away what has been reported is clearly untruthful and implausible; what the leaders feared and sought to prevent by setting guards now becomes their story.[25] Since the Roman governor had been involved in the initial request, the leaders assure the soldiers that they will "fix" it with him, not a new event (27:20), and keep them out of trouble. "The episode presents the leaders in the worst possible light."[26] The soldiers accept the money and follow instructions.

The evangelist then reflects that this story is still doing the rounds with the Jewish people at the time of his writing.[27] Clearly, this is an issue for his church, and Matthew seeks to show that the tale is groundless.[28] There are two stories in circulation; both admit that the tomb was empty, one claiming that this is because the body of Jesus was raised to life by God, the other maintaining that the body was stolen by the disciples and a deception was involved. "Matthew's Christians are living in the truth of the risen Jesus, while the Jews are living and telling a lie."[29] And the responsibility for this untruth lies with the Jewish leadership.

The Mountain Appearance

Introduction

Matthew's Gospel closes with the appearance of the risen Jesus to his disciples on a mountain in Galilee and his sending them on mission to the world (28:16–20). Like most good stories, the Gospel reaches its climax at the end. This brief scene, often referred to as 'The Great Commission', forms a very impressive finale; it is the high point of the whole Gospel narrative, the goal towards which the action and the story have been moving. It provides the interpretive key which unlocks the meaning of the whole book[30] and reveals the core of Matthew's message, his presentation of the person and role of Jesus, and his understanding of the nature of Christian discipleship. It can serve as a summary of the whole Gospel.[31]

In the Gospels there are a number of resurrection narratives, and they tend to follow a common pattern or template:[32] a situation is described in which the disciples, bereft of their Master, are despondent and fearful; Jesus suddenly becomes present; there is some form of greeting by Jesus and an indication of hesitancy and non-recognition on the part of the disciples; then comes the climax, the moment of recognition; finally, Jesus sends them forth on mission. While most of these elements are present in Matthew's narrative, the emphasis is clearly on the commissioning, which is highly developed and thoroughly Matthean in its style, vocabulary and theological standpoint.[33] The episode reads as follows:

Now the eleven disciples went to Galilee, to the mountain to which Jesus had directed them. When they saw him, they worshipped him; but some doubted. And Jesus came and said to them, "All authority in heaven and on earth has been given to me. Go therefore and make disciples of all nations, baptizing them in the name of the Father and of the Son and of the Holy Spirit, and teaching them to obey everything that I have commanded you. And remember, I am with you always, to the end of the age." (28: 16–20)

This concluding section of the Gospel can be structured in the following way, with two main sections:

1) 16–18a: narrative (containing the first four points of the pattern)
2) 18b–20: the message of the risen Jesus:
   • 18b: announcement of exaltation (as a past event)
   • 19–20a: the commissioning:
     — make disciples
     — baptise
     — teach
   • 20b: the promise of Jesus' continuing sustaining presence.

In summary, after the death and resurrection, which for Matthew is the pivotal turning point of history, Jesus comes to his disciples as the glorious Son of Man to found and commission his church, sending it to all peoples (not restricting it to the Jews), with baptism not circumcision as the initiation rite, and with his commands, not the Mosaic Law, as the final norm of morality. And Jesus assures his disciples that he will remain with them (as Emmanuel, God-with-us) as they seek to live out their mission and discipleship.[34] Tom Wright comments that these final verses, in which Jesus meets his followers, gather up the whole gospel and pack it tight. We need to ponder each line and phrase.[35] And that is what we shall do!

The Narrative 28:16–18a

Meanwhile the eleven disciples set out for Galilee, to the mountain where Jesus had arranged to meet them.

This is the only time that Matthew refers to the group of disciples as the "eleven". It is a poignant reminder of the failure and fate of Judas, and of the passion of Jesus. In setting out for Galilee, they are following the instructions of Jesus to the women at the tomb (28:10); Jesus and the angel before him (28:7) had promised that the disciples, his "brothers", would see him in Galilee.[36] This promise is about to reach its fulfilment. Matthew, Mark and John 21 follow the tradition that locates the primary appearance of Jesus in Galilee, the place where Jesus' ministry began, where the disciples were called and where Jesus had experienced a positive response.[37] The other tradition, found in Luke and John 20, locates the appearance in Jerusalem. The Galilee tradition is thought to be probably the more likely from a historical perspective.[38]

The Galilee location is also of theological significance. In 4:15, as Jesus inaugurates his ministry, Isaiah's reference to "Galilee of the nations" is recalled. Galilee is now the symbolic starting point of the mission to all the nations, the light coming to those in darkness, indicating the fulfilment of that prophetic text.[39] Neither Jesus nor the angel had mentioned meeting up on a mountain, but throughout the Gospel narrative, mountains play an important role: the third temptation story (4:1–11), the prayer of Jesus alone on a mountain (14:23), the multiple healings (15:29), the transfiguration (17:1–13), the great sermon where the new Moses gives the new people the new law (5:1 ff). As in the Old Testament, mountains are places of revelation, where the divine and the human can meet. Mount Sinai was the focal point of God's revelation and law-giving to Moses, the location where the creation of the covenanted people took place. Now the great revelation that the Kingdom has begun is about to take place in this unidentified mountain setting.[40] It is interesting that throughout this episode Matthew uses Jesus' name simply, without any title. Alongside the Galilee setting, this is a subtle way of indicating the identity between the Jesus of the ministry and the risen Lord.

When they saw him they fell down before him, though some hesitated. (28:17)

The evangelist does not provide many details in his description of the appearance; the focus of his interest is not so much the appearance as what Jesus will say. The arrival of the risen One is not stated explicitly; the text does not say "he appeared"; he comes not in heavenly splendour, but simply as Jesus.[41] In a subordinate clause, the disciples are said to see him, as promised in 28:10. The language of seeing is typical of the resurrection narratives, and also of the early tradition as recorded by Paul in 1 Corinthians 15. It is not to be understood as indicating physical sight in the same way as we experience it.

The gesture of the disciples in falling down before him (proskynein), which is the main verb in this sentence, is one of adoration, of worship; it indicates the correct reaction, an attitude of faith. The verb is used of the Magi in the Infancy Narrative (2:11), and of the disciples themselves after the incident of the calming of the storm and walking on the water (14:33), and of the women at the tomb. The emphasis is on this response rather than on the appearance itself.[42] It suggests that they recognised him and believed that he had risen.[43]

The element of doubt or hesitation is a feature of the Resurrection Narrative pattern; it is personified in Thomas in John's story.[44] It highlights the unexpectedness of the encounter, and also the change which has taken place. Jesus is the same, but different. There is continuity, but also transformation. The detail probably comes from the early tradition, and Matthew mentions it because it is part of the original story. It is not clear whether he means that some disciples believe, and others doubt, or whether all were hesitant and uncertain.[45] He does not deal explicitly with the resolution of their doubt, as his interest is in the words of Jesus. The fact that they all receive Jesus' mandate and the assurance of his supportive presence implies the dissipation of their doubt and their coming to faith.[46]

This is a paradigm of what discipleship always means: believers caught between adoration and doubt; people believe and yet can falter in their belief. The hesitation is practical oscillation rather than doctrinal difficulty.[47] Perhaps Matthew included the detail because he wanted his community to apply it to themselves; there were "men of little faith" in his community, as is evident from the parables of the dragnet (13:47), and the sheep and goats (25:31). "Faith is not a facile response."[48] It is clear from 1 Corinthians 15 that the early Church had to wrestle with doubt; Matthew's community was not the first in which such a problem arose. It can be a struggle for any disciple. The doubt will be overcome by the message of the risen One, and by obedience to his word.

Jesus came up and spoke to them.

With echoes of the transfiguration account (17:7), Jesus takes the initiative and simply draws near to them graciously, as they lie prostrate, and re-establishes a relationship with them.[49] There is no rebuke; rather, he speaks words of comfort and commissioning.

The Words of Jesus (28:18b–20)

He said, "All authority in heaven and on earth has been given to me."

In Matthew's Gospel there is no separate account of the ascension/exaltation of Jesus. His understanding, not unlike that found in other New Testament strands, is that through the resurrection Jesus has received from the Father universal, total and eternal dominion; the verb "has been given" is in the passive, indicating divine agency. Vindicated by God, he now belongs to the divine sphere; he has been enthroned as messianic king in power. All the authority and dignity which in the tradition of Judaism belonged only to Yahweh now resides in him.[50]

This picture recalls the figure in the book of Daniel (7:14), the all-powerful Son of Man, who is endowed with cosmic authority.[51] Jesus is the Son of Man, already established as the eschatological judge and ruler. Whereas the earthly Jesus had authority, now he has "all" authority.[52] The resurrection has ushered in a period when Jesus is Lord of the cosmos (the verb is in the aorist tense). Jesus' status is now different; a new situation has begun. The temptation scene is now reversed; there Jesus was content to be servant, and his faithfulness was costly, but now he has prerogatives higher than the rule of all earthly kingdoms. "He already possesses the power which he will exercise on earth prior to and in anticipation of his parousia,"[53] his second coming. During his trial Jesus had told Caiaphas: "From now on you will see the Son of Man seated at the right hand of Power" (26:64). This anticipated coming is experienced in the church, where the Kingdom is a subjectively appropriated experience, the only place where the Son of Man both rules and is acknowledged.[54]

Go, therefore, make disciples of all nations; (28:19a)

The "therefore" indicates that what follows is clearly a consequence of the previous saying. The commissioning of the disciples is linked to the power and authority of Jesus as the exalted one. The verb "make disciples" is in the imperative; the subsequent verbs (baptising, teaching) are participles with a mandatory force. Rather than adopt the language of proclaiming the good news, Matthew gives his own characteristic nuance, using a word he has used before (13:53; 27:57). Throughout the Gospel he has devoted much attention to explaining what discipleship means, especially the idea of doing God's will.[55] Nurturing discipleship is the main focus of mission, as other people are caught up in learning from Jesus through them.[56]

Earlier in the Gospel narrative, Jesus sent the disciples on mission, but restricted their work to the Jews, "the lost sheep of the house of Israel" (10:5; 15:24); this restriction is now rescinded. The 'Old Age' has been shattered by the resurrection, the 'Last Days' have come. In Isaiah the wall of Jewish exclusiveness was breached by the image of the Gentiles coming to Sion in the last days (Isa 2:1–4). Now the disciples are to move out, and all peoples are to be invited to submit to the rule of the Son of Man. Jesus is indeed the Son of Abraham in whom the nations are blessed, as Matthew heralded in the Infancy Narrative; Jesus died "for the many", which means for everyone (26:28). This is probably the most explicit statement of the universal mission of the Church anywhere in the New Testament. While the first community's witnesses to the resurrection understood their encounter with the risen Jesus from the outset as involving a responsibility to spread the Good News to others, it proved to be a struggle before the idea of a Gentile mission came to be accepted. This suggests that the risen Jesus did not give so explicit and direct a command for a universal Gentile mission, but that these words were placed in his mouth by the Church when it had come to learn and to experience the universal nature of its message. The Church, for Matthew, is essentially a missionary Church.[57] However, the possibility of the salvation of pagans was suggested by the words and actions of Jesus in the ministry (8:11; 15:21–28).[58]

Another issue that scholars discuss is whether the injunction of Jesus includes Israel among the many nations, or refers exclusively to Gentiles, implying that the mission to the Jews is over. The former is the majority opinion; the Gospel suggests an ongoing mission (10:23), and the majority of Matthew's community were Jews; but Matthew probably did not entertain great hopes of success.[59]

Baptising them in the name of the Father and of the Son and of the Holy Spirit.

Baptism is the way in which a person transfers from being an unbeliever to becoming a disciple. Public and visible, it is envisaged as the initiation rite by means of which the Christian community separates itself and its members from any other community, especially the Jewish community. "Christians now have a physical means of defining themselves as a community, a symbolic act which gives them identity as a community."[60]

Only here is baptism said to have been explicitly instituted and commanded by Jesus. Clearly baptism was practised from the very outset of the Christian mission in its Palestinian/Aramaic speaking stage, where it was understood as proleptic or anticipated participation in the eschatological Kingdom of God through forgiveness of sins and the gift of the Spirit (a derivation from John's baptism). When the Gentile mission was undertaken, baptism came to be seen as participation in Jesus' death and in his resurrection. The early Christian preachers revived the practice of baptism soon after Easter; they probably understood that the call to witness to the Christ event and proclaim the Gospel involved a charge to baptise.[61] Circumcision is not mentioned because it has been replaced. This is a radical step, difficult for Christian Jews to assimilate, and alien to their Jewish neighbours, because circumcision was the sign of uniqueness.[62]

There is frequent reference to "the name" in early Christian hymns; it stands for the person. That Matthew should adopt the term is not remarkable; what is remarkable is this early use of the triadic formula. Elsewhere in the New Testament baptism is described as performed "in the name of Jesus" (Acts 2:38; 8:16; 10:48; 1 Cor 6:11). We find "into Christ Jesus" in Romans 6:3; "into Christ" in Galatians 3:27. Many commentators doubt that the trinitarian formula was original at this point in the gospel, there being no further evidence for it. However, Greek manuscript evidence for the longer text is unanimous. It seems that the monadic form did continue also (Eusebius and other Fathers are aware of it). Trinitarian formulations of a liturgical and doxological character are found in Paul (1 Cor 12:4–6; 1 Cor 6:11; 2 Cor 13:13–14; Gal 4:6; and 1 Pet 1:2). It would seem, then, that the formula arose and came to be used for baptism in Matthew's Church. It is found in the *Didache*, a document thought to be of similar provenance, and so was known by the end of the first century. By 100 CE, the form was established in the Syrian Church, and it came to be used in Rome by 150 CE. Meier holds that the trinitarian formula is not so surprising, given Matthew's high Christology, his emphasis on the personal relationship between Father and Son, and the share which the disciples have in this relationship. It is a forceful proclamation of the divinity of Jesus and the Spirit's distinct personality.[63] Through baptism one is plunged "into" the name of the Trinity, immersed in the bonds of family love binding the three and binding the members of the community. Baptism is incorporation into the life of the Covenant and the Church. It is worth noting that there is no explicit mention of forgiveness of sins.

And teach them to observe all the commands I gave you.

It is interesting that this is the first time that Matthew uses "to teach" as a role of the disciples. In his description of the ministry he often refers to Jesus teaching (4:23; 5:2; 7:29; 9:35; 11:1; 13:34; 21:23; 26:55). When Mark uses the term of Jesus, Matthew follows him. When Mark lacks it (11:28), Matthew adds it (21:23). He avoids it when Mark uses it of the disciples (Mk 6:30;

Matt 14:13). In the missionary charge of 10:1–7, Matthew omits a command to teach. Throughout the Gospel there is great emphasis on Jesus as teacher and on the content of his teaching, as the five major discourses of the Gospel illustrate. This teaching is the new revelation which Jesus gives. "Only after Jesus has completed his teaching, and after the New Age has been inaugurated, does Jesus send his disciples to teach."[64] But Jesus remains the only teacher of his church.[65]

The disciples are commissioned to teach all that Jesus has taught, as presented in the five discourses, (not just the Sermon on the Mount), to hand on his revelation concerning what we should think and do, the attitudes we should have; and Matthew's emphasis on totality shows his preoccupation with leading his community to perfection, a perfection greater than that of Pharisee Judaism. The commands of the earthly Jesus are to be observed as the definitive norm of morality, definitive interpretation of the Law, ultimate criterion for deciding God's will. The Torah, which is becoming the central factor of Judaism after the destruction of the Temple, is now replaced (or perfected).[66] The teaching of Jesus replaces that of Moses. The language here is phrased so as to allude to the Torah ("teach", "observe" "commandments"; see 19:17; 23:3; Deut 5–6, especially 6:1).[67] It is not only a question of Jesus' verbal revelation; his way of living and acting is included.[68]

Perrin concludes that the commission is "to teach and interpret authoritatively the new verbal revelation of God to his people, the tenets of the teaching of Jesus."[69] To live in a world where Jesus is risen is to "accept the privileges and responsibilities of a life lived as response to the new verbal revelation of God to his people through Christ, as this revelation is authoritatively interpreted by the Church specifically commissioned to this task by the risen Jesus himself."[70]

And look, I am with you always; yes, to the end of time.

As this missionary task is daunting, Jesus makes a promise, which is a source of both consolation and strength. It was customary in Judaism to end a book with a blessing and a word of consolation. In the Old Testament, Yahweh always assured those whom he called and sent that he was with them.[71] Now, with a solemn introductory "See" *(idou),* Jesus promises his abiding presence with his nascent Church. The text echoes 1:23: Emmanuel, God with us; that presence of God-in-Christ continues. From a literary point of view this is an inclusion.[72] The theme is found in 8:23, the stilling of the storm, where Matthew's redactional changes turn the episode into an allegory of the

Church. There is the saying in 18:20: "where two or three ...", his presence with the community in prayer.[73] So Jesus' promise points back to the story of Jesus' ministry. Now he will likewise be present with his Church on mission. His presence to his pilgrim Church will be a dynamic, energising, enabling presence.[74] As I have mentioned already, in Matthew there is no mention of departure or ascension; Jesus promises to remain; the exalted Jesus remains present with and through the Church, and fulfils the functions attributed elsewhere in the New Testament to the Holy Spirit.[75] "His struggle to displace the grip of Satan and reclaim the world for the rule (the Kingdom) of God continues as, clad with his authority, the disciples go out on their mission to the nations of the world."[76]

"The end of time" is Matthew's characteristic expression for the end of the world (13:39, 49; 24:3), and it appropriately concludes his Gospel. He sees the resurrection as inaugurating a new age, the world's final age, which is the age of the Church, between the anticipated parousia (resurrection) and the glorious final parousia.[77] But a definite limit is set. The interim is the period of the Church's mission and life. Matthew has thus come to terms with the delay in the parousia by means of his realised eschatology. It is interesting to note the frequent use of "all" in 28:16–20, denoting fullness of power, mission, teaching, time and space.[78] Matthew's Gospel comes to a close with this promise of Jesus. Jesus "remains there, in his word, in his commandments, and in the experience of the presence of God amongst those who hear and do this word."[79]

Conclusion

"The great commission and its frame with which Matthew ends, remain, like the whole Gospel itself, one of the priceless treasures of the Christian Church, providing comfort, strength, and hope until the final dawning of the eschaton."[80] Harrington sees the passage as a summary of the major Christological motifs present throughout the Gospel: Jesus is worthy of worship; he is the teacher; as Son of Man, he has all authority; as Son of God, he directs the disciples to the Gentiles; as Emmanuel, he is present with them. The discipleship theme reaches a climax too, as they believe and are commissioned. The commission is not an ending but a beginning, inviting to discipleship and evangelisation till the final coming of the Son of Man. In the meantime, Jesus has indicated what may happen: persecution leading many to fall away (13:21); a mixture of good and bad within the Church (13:24–30); many will grow weary of waiting

(25:1–13); but he will come to judge the nations (25:31–46).[81] For Matthew, the resurrection inaugurates the age of the Church, a community with a mission in the world.

Reflections

Perhaps, first, we need to acknowledge a negative reminder of things to be avoided, akin to today's 'fake news' craze. Several scholars are scathingly critical of Matthew's addition to the Markan story of the detail concerning the placing of soldiers and the reaction of the authorities to their report. It seems to be an example of fake news created to counter an example of fake news! After the destruction of Jerusalem and the temple by the Romans in 70 CE, the Jewish people, under the leadership of the Pharisees, became a Torah-based community. Clearly the relationship between Judaism and the emerging Christian community was fraught with difficulty, and it appears that the issue of Jesus' resurrection was a source of polemic, with propaganda and counterpropaganda. From our point of view centuries later, the approach of Matthew and his community to this issue leaves much to be desired. If contentious issues emerge in our relationships with other Christian and non-Christian groups, we need to find other ways of handling them, ways which do not compromise truth and respect.

Recent publicity about fake news is perhaps a warning to all of us. Lack of respect for truth and for the human person, especially through misuse of social media, can easily become accepted as normal. It can be quite destructive; it can undermine trust and cause fear and anxiety. The basic fabric of human relating can be severely weakened. As disciples of Jesus we can easily be caught up in this, and we need to be vigilant and self-critical.

The women who go to the tomb receive a much more positive treatment by Matthew than by Mark. Afraid yet joyful, they obediently set off in haste to fulfil the command of the "angel of the Lord", and to communicate to the disciples the Good News that Jesus has been raised from the dead. They are then encountered by the risen Jesus himself, and express their faith and love as they grasp his feet in worship. The message they hear from Jesus contains three key elements. There is no need to be afraid; the disciples are forgiven for their failure, for they are called "my brothers"; and there is the assurance that on returning to Galilee these too will "see" him. Again, we are reminded to lay aside our fears; our failures do not determine our identity in Jesus' eyes. His love, acceptance and mercy embrace us too, and are quite amazing, and deeply reassuring for all of us.

Reflecting on the words of Jesus in the great commission, I cannot but be grateful for the gift of baptism, which drew me into relationship with the risen Jesus, and introduced me into the family of God, the community of the new covenant. Because of this, each of us, as the baptised, with a clear Christian identity, is called to bear witness to and to proclaim and teach the way of Jesus in our daily lives, to make his values, outlook and lifestyle our own, so that the Kingdom may come more completely. This is our daily mission, wherever we are, and whatever the circumstances of our lives, nurturing discipleship.[82] And we are assured of the ongoing presence of Jesus with us day by day, our Emmanuel, until we meet him in glory. This conviction and experience are sources of comfort, hope and strength as we journey on.

Notes

1   Matthew uses Mark as his main source; he also uses other traditions and his own initiative and creativity (Moloney, *Resurrection*, 42). He is thought to have written his Gospel in the final quarter of the first century, probably in Syria, possibly in Antioch. He was probably a Greek-speaking Jewish Christian. His community was in the main composed of Jewish Christians, but Gentile converts were now joining them.

2   Probably the two stages of the story of the guards were originally a connected narrative into which Matthew inserted the scene of the women's visit: Donald A. Hagner, *Matthew*, 2 vols (Nashville: Nelson, 1995), 2,861. John P. Meier, *Matthew* (Dublin: Veritas, 1980), 356–57, notes that the story reflects the arguments about the resurrection between Jews and Christians in the first century; it is the product of Jewish polemics and Christian apologetics, not an eyewitness report. H. Benedict Green, *The Gospel according to Matthew* (Oxford: University Press, 1975), 226, labels the story as Christian counter-propaganda. Francis W. Beare, *The Gospel according to Matthew* (Oxford: Blackwell, 1981), 539, calls it "a christian fabrication" to counter the Jewish assertion that Jesus was not raised from the dead. Ulrich Luz, *Matthew* 3 vols. Translated by James E. Crouch. Hermeneia. (Minneapolis, MN: Fortress, 2001–2007), 3,585–86, sees the section as Matthean

special material, thoroughly Matthean in language; Matthew's purpose is to combat the rumour circulating in the Judaism of his day that the body had been stolen. It is not a historical report, but a polemical legend, a fiction created by Matthew. Dunn, *Jesus Remembered,* 830, believes that the story of the guard is generally regarded an apologetic addition; the difficulty of integrating their presence with the earlier account of the women going to the tomb is obvious, and the reason given for the setting of the guard speaks more of later apologetic concern—perhaps to counter the alternative explanation (the disciples stole the body) already in circulation and still at play at the time of Matthew.

3   For the literary structure, Moloney, *Resurrection,* 43, suggests a "leap-frogging" movement between negative and positive episodes, as during the passion narrative. Luz, *Matthew,* 3, 584, refers to "alternating sections". Brown, *Risen Christ,* 23–24, includes the burial with the other four episodes, so that 1, 3, 5 are favourable to Jesus, 2 and 4 concern people who are hostile. This alternation is present also in the fivefold structure of the Infancy Narrative. William D. Davies and Dale C. Allison, *A Critical and Exegetical Commentary on the Gospel according to Saint Matthew* (London: T&T Clark, 2004), 538, note the parallels between the beginning and ending of the Gospel; they mirror each other. Brendan Byrne, *Lifting the Burden* (Collegeville, MN: Liturgical Press, 2004), 221, also notes the two contrasting themes present in Matthew's presentation of the passion and resurrection of Jesus: the passion was something malevolent human beings did to Jesus; it was also something that God was doing, in the person of the obedient Son, for humankind. This truth is unveiled in the resurrection story.

4   Fuller, *Resurrection Narratives,* 72. Matthew, however, does not highlight this breach of Sabbath observance; he avoids calling this day "the Sabbath." Brown, *Risen Christ,* 27, suggests deliberate irony on Matthew's part.

5   This is the only time that the Pharisees are linked with the chief priests, apart from 21:45, and the first time that they are mentioned in the passion narrative. Prior to the passion they were Jesus' main opponents. Byrne, *Lifting the Burden,* 220, refers to a "relic of anti-Jewish propaganda emanating from the Matthean community." Along with the later story "it has no place in any credible Christian apologetic and no place, consequently, in responsible proclamation of the Gospel." Meier, *Matthew,* 357, suggests that the presence of the Pharisees may be because they were in control of Judaism in Matthew's day, and he wishes to place them at the origin of the lie. Green, *Matthew,* 226, suggests that their addressing Pilate as "Sir" (*Kyrie*), the term used in the Gospel for Jesus or God, indicates that the authorities have now no other lord but Caesar's representative. For Brown, *Risen Christ,* 26, this is Matthean irony.

6   16:21; 17:22-23; 20:17–19. In these texts, when Jesus is speaking to the disciples, Matthew uses "on the third day", rather than "after three days." In 12:40, in responding to the scribes, Jesus speaks about the Son of Man being in the earth for three days and three nights. The text is related to that saying. See also 26:61;

27:40. Fuller, *Resurrection Narratives*, 73, notes that "the third day" reflects the early Christian kerygma, as in 1 Cor 15:4. For the Jewish mind, resurrection was understood as from the grave; the concepts of resurrection and empty tomb were inseparable.

7   These phrases are central to the basic kerygma and proclamation.

8   Meier, *Matthew*, 358, believes it is more likely that Pilate assigns a Roman detachment; the Greek is open to either view. Hagner, *Matthew*, 2, 863, likewise, since the term used is a Latin loanword, and they seem to be answerable to Pilate; Pilate might also wish to forge good relations with the religious leaders. Davies and Allison, *Matthew*, 538, strongly maintain that the soldiers are Roman: in 28:13 the word is the same as 27:27, where they are certainly Roman; 28:14 assumes that they are Pilate's. Brown, *Risen Christ*, 26, clearly opts for Roman soldiers; this means that the secular and religious authorities conspire together against the resurrection, as Herod and the chief priests and scribes did in the Infancy Narrative.

9   For sealing the stone see Josh 10:18; Dan 6:17. Davies and Allison, *Matthew*, 538, note that it is not clear whether a wax seal is intended or a cord. Hagner, *Matthew*, 2, 863, observes that the religious authorities overestimate the disciples, who were not thinking of Jesus' words about resurrection, and "whose psychological condition hardly made it possible for them to perpetrate such a hoax as the Jewish authorities feared." They took Jesus' words more seriously than did the disciples! Davies and Allison, *Matthew*, 538, point out the parallels between the beginning and ending of the Gospel; they mirror each other. Theologically, it is clear that hostility endures. Yet, human efforts are impotent in the face of God's power.

10   Brown, *Risen Christ*, 27.

11   Donald Senior, *Matthew* (Nashville: Abingdon Press, 1998), 340. The apocryphal Gospel of Peter attempts a detailed description (9:35–11, 44). Fuller, *Resurrection Narratives*, 74, states that this is the nearest the canonical Gospels ever come to narrating the actual resurrection. Luz, *Matthew*, 3, 591, asserts that it is generally agreed that Mark is the main source.

12   The Sabbath ran from sunset on Friday to sunset on Saturday.

13   Meier, *Matthew*, 360, notes that Jesus' death and resurrection together form one great eschatological event, "the turning of the ages." Davies and Allison, *Matthew*, 541, see this earthquake as probably having eschatological content: "Jesus' resurrection is an end-time event." Brown, *Risen Christ*, 28, refers to an event of "cosmic importance." Dunn, *Jesus Remembered*, 830, n. 16, sees this as "a Matthean storytelling flourish", indicating the eschatological significance of the event.

14   Matthew is thus clearer than the other evangelists in designating the angelic presence as "the angel of the Lord" (as in the Infancy Narrative), rather than one or two young men. Though these may indeed be angels, Mark and Luke do not specifically say so. The "angel of the Lord" means God in visible form (Meier, *Matthew*, 361). The angel's action is not to be understood as opening the tomb for

Jesus to leave, but to reveal the emptiness of the place. Also David Hill, *The Gospel of Matthew* (London: Oliphants, 1972), 359; Brown, *Risen Christ,* 29. Davies and Allison, 540, note how the angelophany of 28:1-8 mirrors the angel's appearance to Joseph in 1:18-21, 24-25; similarly Brown, *Risen Christ,* 29. Structurally, Luz, 3:591, observes how the angel dominates vv. 2-7; and also refers to the links with the Infancy Narrative.

15   Luz, *Matthew,* 3:596: "God is at work here." Moloney, *Resurrection,* 45-46, notes that Jesus words in 5:17-20 concerning the fulfilment of all the details of the Law and the limitation of the disciples' mission to Israel (10:5-6) have now come to an end, because a new time, a fresh era is dawning. The death and resurrection of Jesus is the turning point of the ages. Senior, *Matthew,* 344, observes that the resurrection marks the beginning of the final age of the world.

16   The early Christian confessions of faith, as we have seen in the Introduction, contained the contrast (antithetical formulas); see 1 Cor 1:23; Gal 3:1.

17   Unlike Mark, there is no specific mention of Peter. Davies and Allison, *Matthew,* 542, suggest that in 28:16–20 Peter is just one of the group.

18   Hagner, *Matthew,* 2, 871, observes that in that culture no invented story would have given women such prominence and entrusted the first proclamation of the resurrection to them. Further, if the tomb had not been empty, it would have been impossible for the church to proclaim the resurrection.

19   Luz, *Matthew,* 3, 598, sees this ambivalence of feeling as characteristic of Matthew's image of a disciple.

20   As Hagner, *Matthew,* 2, 872, puts it: "their message becomes reality."

21   This is a favourite verb for Matthew (*proserchomai*), often used in the ministry for people who come to Jesus for healing or with other requests. The doubt element, a normal aspect of resurrection appearance narratives, is omitted.

22   The verb used is *proskuneō,* which Matthew often uses to indicate the presence of the divine in Jesus' story (see Moloney, *Resurrection,* 47). It is an expression of intimacy and self-subordination. Hagner, *Matthew,* 2, 874, notes that to grasp someone's feet was in that culture an expression of submission and homage. Luz, *Matthew,* 3, 607, calls it an act of veneration (see the Magi in 2:11; sick people in 8:2; 9:18; 15:25; Peter in 14:33). Brown, *Risen Christ,* 31, suggests that the gesture expresses human affection for Jesus.

23   Luz, *Matthew,* 3, 607, comments that although the women's behaviour expresses no fear, Jesus' word is important for Matthew: this is a meeting with a divine being; a meeting with the risen Lord frees them from fear.

24   In this passage there are many points of similarity with John's account of Jesus' appearance to Magdalene. Senior, *Matthew,* 342, nevertheless sees it as a composition of Matthew. Davies and Allison, *Matthew,* 540, note the close similarity

between verses 5-7 and 10, and hold that "the repetition makes for emphasis."
Byrne, *Lifting the Burden*, 222, observes that this encounter seems superfluous,
since Jesus repeats what the angel has said, and an experience of the risen Lord
blunts the impact of the final scene in Galilee. However, it completes the continuity
of the women's faithful witness. Meier, *Matthew*, 364, maintains that the meeting
emphasises that Jesus' risen body is a real body. Instead of titles, Matthew refers to
Jesus as Jesus throughout this chapter. The disciples are forgiven and restored to
fellowship as "brothers". Jesus appears in order to send on mission.

25   Meier, *Matthew*, 365, believes that Matthew intends the lie to be patently
ridiculous. Hagner, *Matthew*, 2. 876, notes the irony that the thing the chief
priests hoped to prevent becomes the story they concoct. To fall asleep was grossly
irresponsible; and if they were asleep they would not have seen what happened!

26   Senior, *Matthew*, 343. Davies and Allison, *Matthew*, 545, comment on the
parallels between chapter 2 and 28:1-15. Similarly, Brown, *Risen Christ*, 32.

27   Meier, *Matthew*, 366, makes the point that Matthew has always spoken
about Israel; now he uses the term "Jews" for the people of the old covenant; they
have lost their privileged status. The kingdom has been taken away from them and
given to a people bearing its fruit, the Church (21:43).

28   Hagner, *Matthew*, 2, 861. Byrne, *Lifting the Burden*, 223, maintains that the
episode is almost certainly a creation of the Matthean community and played a part
in the apologetic of a community struggling for survival in a hostile environment.
Senior, *Matthew*, 343, refers to "polemical encounters" with non-Christian Jewish
groups. Luz, *Matthew*, 3, 611, notes that the Matthew in his fictional story "lays it on
rather thick here." Norman Perrin, *The Resurrection Narratives: A New Approach*
(London: SCM, 1977), 49, sees it as an apologetic legend designed to meet the
calumny that the disciples stole the body. Brown, *Risen Christ*, 32-33, sees it as a
reflection of popular early Christian prejudice.

29   Moloney, *Resurrection*, 49.

30   Meier, *Matthew*, 367. See also Davies and Allison, *Matthew*, 545.

31   Daniel Harrington, *The Gospel of Matthew*, Sacra Pagina 1 (Collegeville,
MN: Liturgical Press, 1991), 416. Davies and Allison, *Matthew*, 548, note that one
cannot improve on 28:16-20; nothing is superfluous, yet seemingly nothing more
could be added without spoiling the effect. It is almost a compendium of Matthean
theology (they provide a list of 11 points). On p. 549, they speak of the passage as
"climax and crown".

32   Brown, *Bodily Resurrection*, 107; this is the concise narrative pattern
discussed by C. H. Dodd, 'The Appearances of the Risen Christ: An Essay in Form-
Criticism of the Gospels' in *Studies in the Gospels*, ed. D.E.Nineham (R. H. Lightfoot
volume; Oxford: Oxford University Press, 1957), 9-35; see also *The Founder of
Christianity*, 175.

44

33   Harrington, *Matthew*, 415, maintains that in all likelihood Matthew himself composed the passage. Some inspiration is to be found in Dan 7:14; other prototypes suggested are Exod 19–20; Num 6:22–27; 2 Chr 36:26. Senior too, *Matthew*, 344, believes that Matthew composed the scene as the finale to his Gospel and as a summary of its most fundamental motifs. He suggests the same Old Testament background as Harrington. Hagner, *Matthew*, 881, lists similarities or points of contact with traditions in Luke, Mark and John (Lk 24:47: proclaiming forgiveness to the nations; 24:38: doubting; 24:52: worship. Mk 16:14: eleven; 16:15: commission to the world; 16:17: in my name. Jn 20:21–23: peace, sending, forgiveness; 14:23: keeping Jesus' word, abiding). While it is clear that Jesus' words are recast in Matthew's style and vocabulary, this does not demonstrate that Matthew composed it *ex nihilo*. He may have worked over a tradition available to him. Meier, *Matthew*, 376, writes that the present form of the pericope comes from Matthew's hand and reflects his theology, although we can discern traces of earlier traditions, perhaps even a tradition about an Easter appearance, which Matthew is adapting for his purposes. Fuller, *Resurrection Narratives*, 82, concludes that the setting is a Matthean composition, but he is using earlier material from lists of appearances. Luz, *Matthew*, **3**, 617, suggests that there was a pre-Matthean appearance story and tradition, which, linguistically, has been reformulated by Matthew. Probably Matthew put together Jesus' concluding word, in part from elements already available to him from his own Gospel.

34   Meier, *Matthew*, 367; Moloney, *Resurrection*, 49, stresses that the signs which marked the death and resurrection (the earthquake and the opening of graves) indicate that heaven and earth are passing away and that all is accomplished (5:18). On p. 50, he observes that the key to understanding this pericope is to see the death and resurrection of Jesus as the turning point of the ages.

35   N. Tom Wright, *Matthew for Everyone*, 2 vols (London: SPCK, 2002), **2**, 205.

36   See also 25:32, Jesus' words on the way from the Supper to the Mount of Olives: "After I am raised up, I will go ahead of you to Galilee."

37   Luz, *Matthew*, **3**, 21.

38   See the final chapter of this book.

39   Byrne, *Lifting the Burden*, 225, notes the pattern in the Gospel whereby Jesus "withdraws" in the face of hostility (2:22; 12:15; 14:13; 15:21). After rejection by the leadership and execution, this is the last instance of that pattern. Luz, **3**, 621 sees a repetition of 2:22, Galilee as a land of refuge.

40   Dunn, *Jesus Remembered*, 853, n. 116, believes that Matthew evidently intended the "mountain" to be understood as the place where divine revelation is given. Moloney, *Resurrection*, 52, stresses the link with the Sermon on The Mount: Jesus there speaks of living perfectly the Law and Prophets until heaven and earth pass away. Through the death and resurrection, one era has come to perfection and

another is about to start. Luz, *Matthew*, 3, 621–22, mentions associations with the mount of temptation, the mountain of the sermon, the transfiguration.

41 Byrne, *Lifting the Burden*, 226. Meier, *Matthew*, 368, comments that the only "title" accorded to Jesus is "Jesus", stressing the identity of the risen One with the earthly Jesus.

42 Harrington, *Matthew*, 414; Luz, *Matthew*, 3, 616.

43 Hagner, *Matthew*, 884.

44 John 20:24–29. Davies and Allison, *Matthew*, 546, point out that failure to see is also an aspect of Old Testament stories: e.g. Joseph's brothers in Gen 42:8.

45 Harrington, *Matthew*, 414, notes that from a grammatical point of view it seems that some worshipped and others doubted. Byrne, *Lifting the Burden*, 226, n. 2, favours this view; also, Hill, *Matthew*, 361: "the worship of the group was not without an element of questioning and hesitation". Senior, *Matthew*, 345, comments that it is unclear whether some or all doubted; he suggests that the meaning may be that the disciples worshipped Jesus yet remained weak and hesitant in this moment of their first encounter with him. Hagner, *Matthew*, 2, 884–5, discusses this at length; he opts for them being hesitant, indecisive; it was too much to assimilate; they were uncertain about what the recent events meant, and what might happen next. Perhaps Matthew included the detail because he wanted his community to apply it to themselves. Luz, **3**, 623, believes that the ambivalence of the disciples is part of Mathew's concept of "little faith", which is not conquered by Jesus once and for all; it happens over and over. Jesus "lets his disciples remain in their conflictedness and turns to them with his word."

46 Wright, *Matthew*, 2, 643–644, sees this item of doubt as a strong mark of authenticity.

47 Meier, *Matthew*, 369.

48 Brown, *Risen Christ*, 34.

49 The term used for Jesus' approach (*proselthein*) is used of Jesus also in the transfiguration significantly; frequently (some fifty times), it is used in the ministry to describe sick people coming to Jesus. (See Beare, *Matthew*, 544).

50 Moloney, *Resurrection*, 52. Hagner, *Matthew*, 2, 886, notes that Jesus refers to his authority in 9:6; 11:27. Now the glorious identity of Jesus becomes plain. Davies and Allison, *Matthew*, 546, observe that several New Testament Christological hymns express the conviction that through the resurrection Jesus is exalted, enthroned and made Lord of the cosmos (Eph 1:20–23; Phil 2:6–11; Col 1:15–20; 1 Pet 3:18–22); similarly, Byrne, *Lifting the Burden*, 227, n. 3. Fuller, *Resurrection Narratives*, 83, refers to its hymn-like character.

51   Dan 7:14 reads: "To him was given dominion and glory and kingship, that all peoples, nations and languages should serve him." Harrington, *Matthew*, 414, notes this too; Senior, *Matthew*, 346; Green, 231; Hagner, *Matthew*, 2, 886; Davies and Allison, *Matthew*, 546. On p.549, they observe that this allusion wraps up the plot in splendid fashion, scripture is fulfilled, and the word of Jesus vindicated (24:30; 26:64). Wright, *Matthew*, 2, 643, sees the "all authority ..." words as a fulfilment of the Lord's prayer concerning the Kingdom; Luz, *Matthew*, 3, 624, with the third petition.

52   Luz, *Matthew*, 3, 624, recalls Gospel texts which refer to the "power" of Jesus: he taught "with power" (7:29); the "power to forgive" (9:6, 8); questioned about it (21:23–27); granted it to the apostles (10:1); and especially 11:27: everything delivered to him by the Father.

53   Perrin, *Resurrection*, 50. Luz, *Matthew*, 3, 625, notes that the power is that of the Son of Man who came to serve.

54   Meier, *Matthew*, 370.

55   Moloney, *Resurrection*, 53, notes that Matthew very frequently uses the term "disciple" (*mathētēs*), which means one who engages in learning through instruction from another. Hagner, *Matthew*, 2, 887, speaks of "nurturing". Byrne, *Lifting the Burden*, 227–228, sees Matthew's Gospel as a handbook for the formation of these new disciples; also, Hagner, *Matthew*, 2, 888. Beare, *Matthew*, 545, suggests that discipleship means renunciation of all earthly ambition, the denial of self, the bearing of the cross, the willingness to be servant of all, the commitment to doing the will of the Father.

56   Hagner, *Matthew*, 2, 887, refers to "the arduous task of nurturing into the experience of discipleship."

57   Luz, *Matthew*, 3, 628.

58   Harrington, *Matthew*, 416, observes that the command to go to the Gentiles may well have carried a message to Matthew's community, marking a new chapter in their history. "The church and the synagogue in Matthew's area are thus on the way to definitive separation." Beare, *Matthew*, 545, comments that this charge is a relatively late formulation; the controversy over the admission of Gentiles to the Christian community is over and forgotten.

59   Moloney, *Resurrection*, 53. Senior, *Matthew*, 347, thinks a continuing mission to the Jews is not forbidden, but a new concentration on Gentiles is inaugurated. For Byrne, *Lifting the Burden*, 227, n. 5, while there is no reason that Israel should not be included, the impression from the Gospel is that for the Matthean community the mission to Israel is factually finished; Israel has largely said 'no'. Hagner, *Matthew*, 2, 887, states that the Jews are not excluded; similarly, Davies and Allison, *Matthew*, 547; Brown, *Risen Christ*, 36. For Meier, *Matthew*, 371, the Jews are not excluded, but no longer enjoy a privileged status as the chosen people. Luz, *Matthew*, 3, 631, believes that the command is fundamentally universal, and

does not exclude a continuing mission to Israel, but Matthew probably has no great hopes for it.

60   Perrin, *Resurrection*, 51.

61   Fuller, *Resurrection Narratives*, 85–86.

62   Moloney, *Resurrection*, 54–55. Wright, *Matthew*, 2, 644, sees baptism as a worldwide extension of the movement of covenant renewal started by John, now continuing under the authority of the risen Jesus and in the power of the Spirit. Byrne, *Lifting the Burden*, 228, n. 3, notes that Matthew, like Paul, holds that Gentile converts do not need to become Jews first in order to enter the renewed People of God.

63   Meier, *Matthew*, 371. Byrne, *Lifting the Burden*, 228, notes the "trinitarian moment" at Jesus' baptism, as the Spirit descends, and the Father's voice is heard. Through baptism we are drawn into that same divine-human communion as God's beloved sons and daughters.

64   Meier, *Matthew*, 372. Perrin, *Resurrection*, 52–54, notes how from chapter 13 onwards, Matthew emphasises how Jesus teaches his disciples, almost exclusively.

65   Luz, *Matthew*, 3, 633. On p. 834, he states that Matthew understands the Church as Jesus' family that does the will of the Father and stands under Jesus' blessing.

66   Moloney, *Resurrection*, 55, states that the Torah is not replaced but perfected (5:17–18). Others prefer replaced.

67   Meier, *Matthew*, 372, writes that the teaching of Jesus encompasses much of what was in the Mosaic Law. But the Church teaches these commands not because they come from Moses, but because they come from Jesus. He suggests that proclamation, baptism, instruction may reflect the process used in Matthew's Church. For Moloney, *Resurrection*, 56, the Law is from now on interpreted through the teaching of Jesus. For Beare, *Matthew*, 545, the teaching is not primarily doctrinal but ethical.

68   Davies and Allison, *Matthew*, 547: word and deed are unified; the entire book is in view.

69   Perrin, *Resurrection*, 55.

70   Perrin, *Resurrection*, 55.

71   See Gen 28:15; Exod 3:12; Josh 1:5,9; Isa 41:10.

72   Harrington, *Matthew*, 415.

73   Other examples of the earthly Jesus' helping presence include: 8:23–27; 14:13–21, 22–23; 15:29–39; 17:1–8; 26:26–29.

74   Meier, *Matthew*, 373.

75   Harrington, *Matthew*, 415, writes that in Matthew the risen Jesus fulfils the functions attributed elsewhere in the New Testament to the Holy Spirit. For Senior, *Matthew*, 348, the risen Jesus himself is the equivalent to the divine presence within the community as it moves out into history. Green, *Matthew*, 232, believes that although Matthew has no explicit thought of the Holy Spirit as accomplishing this presence, the experiential reality which Spirit language expresses is present to his mind.

76   Byrne, *Lifting the Burden*, 229.

77   Perrin, *Resurrection*, 59, maintains that for Matthew and his Church the parousia is no longer regarded as imminent, so the Church becomes the central focus. It is in the Church that one finds the presence of the risen Lord. Moloney, *Resurrection*, 57, recalls that during the ministry, Jesus suggests what will happen during this interim period: persecution, a mixture of good and bad within the Church, weariness in waiting.

78   Wright, *Matthew*, **2**, 645, refers to two age chronology; the age to come has been launched by Jesus' resurrection; the risen Jesus represents and embodies this new age; he becomes the human bridge between it and the present one.

79   Luz, *Matthew*, **3**, 635.

80   Hagner, *Matthew*, **2**, 889.

81   Moloney, *Resurrection*, 57.

82   To use the terminology of Hagner, *Matthew*, **2**, 887.

Chapter Three
The Resurrection in Luke

The situation in Luke's Gospel "on the first day of the week" is less bleak than that which we discussed in Mark.[1] For the darkness shrouding Calvary is offset by the atmosphere of peace and calm that accompanies the death of Jesus, whose final words express his resigned trust in his Father: "Father, into your hands I commit my spirit." On that day after the Sabbath, the Father dramatically reverses Jesus' rejection by the religious elite and the Romans; his messianic vocation, which entailed his passion and death, is clarified and vindicated. For Luke, the various aspects of the Easter event take place on the same day in and around Jerusalem, where Luke's story of Jesus began (1:8–23): the finding of the empty tomb, the Emmaus journey, the final meeting of Jesus with his disciples during a meal in a room in the city and finally, his ascension into heaven.[2] The rehabilitation of the disciples sets the scene for Luke's book of Acts, which describes the beginnings of their mission to the world.

The Empty Tomb (24: 1–12)

The Easter story, the greatest reversal and surprise of the many recounted by Luke, begins on Sunday morning:

> But on the first day of the week, at early dawn, they came to the tomb, taking the spices that they had prepared. They found the stone rolled away from the tomb, but when they went in, they did not find the body. While they were perplexed about this, suddenly two men in dazzling clothes stood beside them. The women were terrified and bowed their faces to the ground, but the men said to them, "Why do you look for the living among the dead? He is not here but has risen.

Remember how he told you, while he was still in Galilee, that the Son of Man must be handed over to sinners, and be crucified, and on the third day rise again." Then they remembered his words, and returning from the tomb, they told all this to the eleven and to all the rest. Now it was Mary Magdalene, Joanna, Mary the mother of James, and the other women with them who told this to the apostles. But these words seemed to them an idle tale, and they did not believe them. But Peter got up and ran to the tomb; stooping and looking in, he saw the linen cloths by themselves; then he went home, amazed at what had happened. (24:1–12)

Luke does not mention by name the women who "had followed him from Galilee" and were present on Calvary, standing at a distance, watching. Nor does he name them when describing the burial of Jesus by Joseph, who, "though a member of the council had not agreed with their action", and who "was waiting expectantly for the kingdom of God." On leaving the Calvary scene the women prepared spices and ointments, and then rested on the Sabbath "in accordance with the commandment" (23:56).³ They are named by Luke only towards the end of the events at the tomb.

At first light "on the first day of the week", our Sunday morning, the women make their way to the tomb. They bring with them the spices which they have already prepared so as to fittingly complete the funeral rites of Jesus as an expression of their love. Their focus is a dead body. On arriving, however, they find to their surprise that the stone has been rolled away. This stone is not mentioned in Luke's account of the burial. They immediately enter the tomb, clearly expecting to find the body of Jesus which they have come to anoint with their spices.⁴ But the body is no longer there, which leaves them perplexed and puzzled.

At this point two men in dazzling apparel, the clothes of the heavenly realm,⁵ appear and stand beside them, and this terrifies them. They bow their faces to the ground or fall prostrate in an expression of reverence and awe.⁶ Without the traditional exhortation not to be afraid, the two in unison immediately address the issue, first with a reproachful question: "Why do you look for the living among the dead?" And then, continuing with the Easter kerygma, they announce the amazing news: "He is not here, but has been raised."⁷ They go on to remind the women of Jesus' words while in Galilee, words which they had heard when in his company there, and ought to have remembered, namely, that he "must" be handed over to sinful people, be crucified, and on the third day rise again. Suffering and vindication go together and are aspects of God's will ("must").[8] Perhaps this is an implicit rebuke for the women.[9]

However, they now remember these words of Jesus; remembering includes a nuance of understanding and insight.[10] They leave the tomb, and without being ordered to do so, they spontaneously pass this message on "to the eleven and to all the rest", which indicates a wider group of disciples. They communicate what they have seen and heard and its significance. They are therefore the first people to believe and to proclaim the resurrection of Jesus.[11] At this point, Mary Magdalene, Joanna, and Mary the mother of James are named; the others accompanying them remain anonymous.[12] The response of the disciples to their news is a refusal to believe, for their message seemed "an idle tale." The tense of the verb suggests an ongoing refusal, even though they knew the women well. The Greek (lēros) means the demented ramblings of someone who is sick.[13] If the women recalled Jesus' words in Galilee, the disciples ought to have been able to do so too, even if at that time they were unable to grasp his meaning, despite being told to "let these words sink into your ears" (9:44). Much more is required to bring them to belief.

Luke's story contains a further element, for Peter runs to the tomb, stoops down and looks in. He perceives the linen cloths, and is amazed at what he observes, which confirms the women's claims, but amazement does not imply faith. Peter returns "home", still unbelieving and failing to grasp what is happening, but perhaps a little more open for what will follow.[14] As readers we are left in suspense, aware than an empty tomb is not in itself an indication of resurrection, but, because of the angels' message, expecting a sequel.

The Emmaus Journey (24:13–35)

The Emmaus story is one of the most beautiful narratives in the New Testament. It is an exquisite masterpiece in which Luke's theological and artistic talents are seen at their finest, "a gem of literary art".[15] Dominating Luke's Easter narrative,[16] it takes up again the themes of the journey, the meal and mercy, themes prominent in Luke's telling of the Gospel story.[17] The fivefold scheme mentioned early in the last chapter provides a useful framework for our reflections.[18]

> Now on that same day two of them were going to a village called Emmaus, about seven miles from Jerusalem, and talking with each other about all these things that had happened. While they were talking and discussing, Jesus himself came

near and went with them, but their eyes were kept from recognizing him. And he said to them, "What are you discussing with each other while you walk along?" They stood still, looking sad. Then one of them, whose name was Cleopas, answered him, "Are you the only stranger in Jerusalem who does not know the things that have taken place there in these days?" He asked them, "What things?" They replied, "The things about Jesus of Nazareth, who was a prophet mighty in deed and word before God and all the people, and how our chief priests and leaders handed him over to be condemned to death and crucified him. But we had hoped that he was the one to redeem Israel. Yes, and besides all this, it is now the third day since these things took place. Moreover, some women of our group astounded us. They were at the tomb early this morning, and when they did not find his body there, they came back and told us that they had indeed seen a vision of angels who said that he was alive. Some of those who were with us went to the tomb and found it just as the women had said; but they did not see him." Then he said to them, "Oh, how foolish you are, and how slow of heart to believe all that the prophets have declared! Was it not necessary that the Messiah should suffer these things and then enter into his glory?" Then beginning with Moses and all the prophets, he interpreted to them the things about himself in all the scriptures.

As they came near the village to which they were going, he walked ahead as if he were going on. But they urged him strongly, saying, "Stay with us, because it is almost evening and the day is now nearly over." So he went in to stay with them. When he was at the table with them, he took bread, blessed and broke it, and gave it to them. Then their eyes were opened, and they recognized him; and he vanished from their sight. They said to each other, "Were not our hearts burning within us while he was talking to us on the road, while he was opening the scriptures to us?" That same hour they got up and returned to Jerusalem; and they found the eleven and their companions gathered together. They were saying, "The Lord has risen indeed, and he has appeared to Simon!" Then they told what had happened on the road, and how he had been made known to them in the breaking of the bread.

The story begins on the first day of the week. In fact, in Luke's Gospel everything takes place on that "day". The two disciples are making their way home after the Passover festival to the village of Emmaus, about seven miles from Jerusalem; the location of this village is uncertain.[19] Some scholars suggest that they may be man and wife, if Cleopas is the same person as the Clopas mentioned in John's version of the Calvary scene as the mother of one of the Mary's present (John 19:25).[20] As they walk along leaden-footed, they share the depths of their distress and disappointment. As so often happens in situations of grief and bereavement, they recall what has taken place, retrace familiar contours, in an attempt to keep the person alive, clinging in tight-gripped desperation to a past which had meaning, and which brought joy and love. We sense the tragedy and poignancy of their situation, the pained brokenness of shattered dreams, articulated later in the story: "Our hope had been that he would be the one to set Israel free." We detect the tones of anguish, bitterness and near despair, and glimpse the empty void which is their future.

A significant factor in the setting for the story is that the two disciples are travelling *away* from Jerusalem. A salient feature of Luke's presentation of the ministry of Jesus is his structural emphasis on Jesus' journey up to Jerusalem, clearly inaugurated in 9:51, and continuing until the solemn entry into the city. It is there that the events called in the transfiguration scene Jesus' "departure" or "exodus" (9:31) take place. It is in Jerusalem that the gift of the Spirit will be bestowed. It is from that city that the apostles will set forth on another journey in mission to the nations. Yet these disciples are walking away; they have turned their backs; they have thrown in the towel; they have abandoned their friends and God's sacred story.[21] As we learn later, they have even heard the women's tale of the empty tomb and angelic vision with its Easter proclamation, but they are walking away in grief and unbelief, hopes shattered, expectations in pieces.

As they walk, the two disciples are engaged in deep conversation, a spirited debate.[22] Then, suddenly, a stranger is walking with them, as the risen Jesus takes the initiative and breaks through, unannounced and unexpected, into the shredded web of their lives and into the midst of their tragedy. When he asks about the topic of their discussion,[23] they stand still, their sadness obvious. Then they avidly seize on his ignorance as simply a visitor to the city,[24] and capitalise on the opportunity to tell their story all over again. He listens to their words and to their *angst,* listens with compassion and understanding, lives with them their questioning bewilderment. He is content to wait, prompting them with a question or two to enable them to bring out their problem, not forcing the pace, not rushing in with instant solutions. He walks their way with them along the twisting, dusty road, stopping and starting with their halting rhythm.

But the two disciples fail to recognise him, and their failure is protracted. "Something kept them from seeing who it was."[25] This motif of non-recognition is one of the devices by which the evangelists underline the 'otherness' of Jesus, the radical transformation which has taken place. Its persistence in this story adds considerably to the dramatic effect and suspense. It also serves to illustrate the truth that vision of the risen One is not a human achievement; it is gift, God's free gift.[26]

At this point in the unfolding of the story, Luke very skilfully, and not without considerable irony,[27] puts on the lips of Cleopas a summary of the early Christian kerygma and catechesis (similar to the preaching of Peter and Paul in Acts 2:22–24 and 13:26f).[28] Jesus is described in terms of the popular estimate of him as "a prophet powerful in action and speech before God and the whole people."[29] A brief resume of the Passion follows, with emphasis on the responsibility of the Jewish leaders.[30] Luke's Cleopas goes on to express the hopes which Jesus had aroused in their own hearts that he was, in fact, *the* prophet, the prophet-like-Moses, the liberator of his people—hopes dashed by his untimely death.[31] Finally, he mentions the empty tomb tradition: the women's visit, the absence of the body, the astounding angelic vision and proclamation, the journey to the tomb made by some of the group of disciples[32] in search of corroboration as hope was rekindled and as suddenly snuffed out in scepticism, a scepticism which they apparently shared. They are very much aware of all the events, the facts, but they fail to understand their significance.[33]

Jesus then responds, jolting them initially with a reproach for their obtuse failure to understand God's ways, their slowness of heart.[34] From the Jewish scriptures he provides the key to the recent events: "Was it not necessary that the Christ should suffer before entering into his glory?" Jesus leads them through the Bible (Moses, the Prophets and the Psalms), highlighting the evidence of God's purpose, the links between the scriptures and his vocation and destiny, detecting an underlying common pattern in God's ways which was a foreshadowing of the pattern of his own messianic mission: rejection leading to acceptance, suffering leading to glory.[35] No specific texts are mentioned. Jesus had himself explicitly spoken of this in what are termed the passion predictions (9:22, 44; 18:31–33). Jesus shows them that not only is suffering not incompatible with messianic kingship; it is necessary, for it is God's providential pathway to glory.

So enthralled and taken up are they by the conversation that the miles imperceptibly slip by, and suddenly Jesus and the two disciples find themselves on the outskirts of Emmaus village, probably the couple's home. There is a heightening of suspense. The two are no longer so self-absorbed; they respond to the stranger, concerned for his need. Jesus makes as if to go on,[36] a gesture which evokes that beautiful invitation, almost a demand:[37] "Stay with us, for evening draws on and the day is almost over" (24:29 NEB).

The disciples thus take the initiative in response to Jesus and his words. It is not without significance that Jesus waits to be asked, for he never imposes himself, never forces his friendship; with remarkable sensitivity he reverences our freedom. But once the offer of hospitality is extended, he accepts promptly (see also Rev 3:20; Jn 14:23). Later they sit at table together.[38] Again Jesus is sharing table with people who have failed, but this time they are his failed disciples.[39] Jesus, though the guest, assumes the role of host: "He took the bread, said the blessing; then he broke it and handed it to them." As has happened so often in the ministry, as Luke tells the story, we find Jesus eating with broken people. He reaches out and touches them in their failure and disloyalty, their fragility and inadequacy, and breaks with them the bread of reconciliation and friendship.[40] That outreach and acceptance in table fellowship transforms their understanding and opens their eyes, and, no doubt recalling earlier meals they had shared, at last they recognise him. At this, he vanishes from their midst.

The Emmaus narrative does not conform precisely to the normal pattern of appearance stories in its conclusion, for there is no explicit commissioning. Nevertheless, the sense of mission is strongly in evidence, for the effect of the encounter with the Lord is that the two disciples depart without delay, despite impending darkness, and retrace their route to Jerusalem in order to reach out and share with the others of their band this gladdening news so filled with promise. Having abandoned Jerusalem in disappointment and scepticism, they now return in faith, with a spring in their step and a smile in their eyes, their hearts on fire, to begin afresh, and to bear witness to the resurrection. "Where before they were ex-followers of a dead prophet, now they are followers of the risen Lord."[41]

On their arrival, the two disciples find the Eleven and the rest of the company assembled, and their news is confirmed: "The Lord has been raised and has appeared to Simon." The risen Jesus has in the meantime reached out to Simon in a similar way, extending to him, too, his forgiveness and fellowship, his reconciliation. Simon, the first official witness to the resurrection of Jesus, can now strengthen the faith of the other disciples (22:32). Easter faith has already been born in Jerusalem.[42]

The Appearance to the Group of Disciples (24:36–49)

As the whole company of his followers talk together excitedly about these extraordinary occurrences, Jesus interrupts them as he suddenly appears in their midst, wishing them peace.[43] Their immediate reaction is one of intense fear, panic, and doubt; they think they are seeing a ghost.[44] Jesus asks why they are afraid and doubting, inviting them to look at his hands and feet, even to touch him. The bodily reality of the risen Jesus is emphasised, though not subject to the normal limitations of our humanity in terms of time, space and movement.[45] He is clearly not a disembodied spirit or a ghost! It really is the same Jesus. Joy invades their wonder and disbelief, as they struggle to come to terms with what is happening, which seems too good to be true.[46] Jesus asks whether there is anything to eat and partakes of the grilled fish they provide as a clear indication of his bodily reality; one presumes that the customary bread was also available. Table fellowship is again experienced.[47]

Jesus uses this opportunity at the meal table, in what amounts to a farewell speech, to open the scriptures to them: the Law, the Prophets and the Psalms. What he shared with the Emmaus couple he now expounds to the whole group. Recalling his teaching during the ministry, he reiterates the message that whatever scripture had said about him had to be fulfilled.[48] He opens their minds to a new level of understanding. He specifies two things. First, the scriptures make it clear that the Messiah must suffer and rise from the dead on the third day. Secondly, the Good News of repentance and forgiveness must be proclaimed in his name to all the nations, starting from Jerusalem.[49] Their role or mission, now formalised, is to bear witness to all that has occurred and all that Jesus has explained. Throughout his ministry, they have heard his teaching, been present for his acts of mercy and healing, have now encountered him in his risen state, and have been led to understand the scriptures and grasp God's saving plan. They have themselves experienced this transforming forgiveness so profoundly in table fellowship with him.[50] Finally, he reveals his intention to send upon them what the Father promised, commanding them to stay in Jerusalem until they are clothed with power from on high, the Holy Spirit. Empowered by the Spirit they will be enabled to carry out faithfully their mission of witness and proclamation to the world.[51]

The Ascension (24: 50–53)

Then he led them out as far as Bethany, and, lifting up his hands, he blessed them. While he was blessing them, he withdrew from them and was carried up into heaven. And they worshipped him, and returned to Jerusalem with great joy; and they were continually in the temple blessing God.

Luke's Gospel closes with another journey, as Jesus leads the group out across the Kidron, as he had done before, and up the hill to Bethany.[52] He does not speak again but gives a final blessing and is carried up into heaven, completing his "exodus".[53] His movement is twofold, away from them and up into heaven. This "signifies the finality of Jesus' departure (until the parousia) and Jesus' glorified status."[54] At this the disciples worship him, which is a clear indication that they have finally recognised his true identity. Then they make their way back to the city, as instructed, but do so replete with joy. They are people transformed. From that moment on, they were continually in the temple blessing God, and waiting for the fulfilment of Jesus' final promise. The Gospel ends in the place, setting and atmosphere where it began. The next phase, the phase of mission, will begin there too. Its Spirit-directed unfolding and expanding will be described in Luke's second book, the Acts.[55]

Reflections

This final section of Luke's Gospel is a rich source for our reflection. The women, who approach the tomb of Jesus in order to perform a final act of love for the Master, have their sorrow turned to joy at the message conveyed by the two angelic figures. It is a classic Lukan reversal, a transformation beyond their wildest dreams and expectations, reminiscent of Elizabeth's experience earlier in the story. They listen to the angels' word and remember what Jesus had told them in Galilee. Spontaneously, they rush to tell the eleven and the other members of the group this amazing news. It just has to be shared. Remembering and sharing must be twin aspects of our mission, as is the pervasive joy of it all.

The response of the male disciples, however, makes us pause for thought. It is doubtless true that such disparaging and condescending comments may reflect the culture of the day. But these women had been with them for months, wandering around in Jesus' company. Surely the male disciples could see that the attitude of Jesus was counter-cultural; he treated women with respect, allowing them to be genuine disciples. It is clearly significant that women were the ones to whom he first appeared and were the first to realise that he had been raised and was alive, the first to be placed in a position where they could announce the amazing Good News, which has transformed the world. One of the greatest indictments of our Church is that little has changed over the centuries. We have not come to terms with the mind and heart of Jesus;

we have not really appreciated the true nature of baptism; in developing the clerical domination system we have betrayed the servant, self-giving style of Jesus. Nor have we adjusted to the way society is evolving. This aspect of Luke's story presents a real challenge to us.

And it is probably not only in this area of human experience and relationships that deep-set prejudices and preconceptions beset us. It can be both surprising and disconcerting how they can suddenly surface. Often, we deny their reality; frequently we are unaware of the way they affect our thinking and actions. This is true of individuals of all ages, of groups of all kinds and of nations across the world. If we are to grow as human beings and as Christian disciples, we need to uncover and unpack this shadow side of our personal being and be alert to the pervasive and pernicious prejudices in the groups to which we belong.

The Emmaus story offers us different areas for reflection, conversion and action. It is difficult to avoid the impression that in this wonderful narrative Luke is less concerned with presenting the resurrection of Jesus as a past event than with exploring how the risen Lord is actively present in the life of the community. He is interested in highlighting those aspects and areas of our living where Jesus continues to encounter us today.[56]

First, it is so easy for us to empathise with the Emmaus couple in their loss and bereavement experience, and in their need to talk about their dreams and their pain and disillusionment. We have ourselves been there, too, perhaps frequently. We also "had hoped". At times, our schemes and dreams and plans fall apart. It is a struggle to see meaning in failure or change, oppression or injustice, in loss of any kind. We can feel let down by friends and family, by people in leadership roles, by those we seek to serve and to whom we minister, by the Church, by God. There can be much anger and frustration and hurt within us, and it can linger long.

Luke is assuring us that Jesus is present with us in these situations, in our stumbling and confusion, when we feel 'let down'; he is walking our way alongside us as faithful companion and friend. It is so important to acknowledge our pain and to share our feelings with him in our prayer, to allow him into our messiness and shadows. His strengthening and liberating presence is frequently mediated by others, fellow travellers, who, through their own suffering and journeying, have learned how to 'be with', have learned how to listen, empathise, offer a healing space and the gift of hospitality. It is crucial to be able to trust and share about our disappointments. Some people carry this kind of pain for years and years, and it can affect and infect relationships, decisions, attitudes and ministry.

Secondly, the failure of the disciples to recognise Jesus can stimulate us to ask what it is in ourselves which can hinder the realisation of his presence with us. The disciples seem too depressed, too caught up in their problems and grief. Perhaps their God is too small, their expectations too limited and narrow. They are not open to what is new and unexpected and freely given, to a God of such unfathomable love, a God of surprises. We, too, can at times be bogged down in the rut of routine or the heavy sands of our problems and preoccupations; or we can be just too busy. We can be blinded by our self-centredness or introspection, deafened by the strident sounds inside and around us. Perhaps we are looking for a God fashioned to our own sketchy design; perhaps we are pining for what is tried and comfortable, afraid of letting go, of losing our control and security. Like the Emmaus couple, we can thus be closed to the divine stranger, and he goes unrecognised.

Thirdly, one of the points which the evangelist wishes to teach us through this narrative, and also the later appearance of Jesus to the larger group of disciples, is that in the study and prayerful pondering of scripture the risen Lord is to be encountered, is reassuringly present, deepening our insight and understanding, widening our perspectives, firming up our commitment, disturbing and challenging our lives, "setting our hearts on fire". The risen Jesus is present whenever his life-giving word is proclaimed, the Good News of God's forgiveness, acceptance and faithful love. It is a word which also summons us to model our lives on the messianic pattern of his and to surrender in trust to the mystery of God's loving plan. Today there is much greater interest in reflecting on scripture, in *lectio divina*. Perhaps we need to ask ourselves whether we are indeed people of the word.

In addition, one of the details of the narrative which fascinates me is the change which takes place in the disciples as they listen to Jesus' words. As long as they are concerned exclusively with their own problems and grief and disappointment, their horizons are shrouded in thick cloud. But their focus changes; they begin to look beyond themselves; they see the stranger's need for food and shelter and rest; they open their hearts to the other. The clouds then begin to lift and the sun filters through. In this, I believe that the evangelist is reminding us that the risen Lord is present and can be encountered wherever there is care and service of others, however ordinary and prosaic its mode of expression might be. Selflessness can open our eyes so that we may catch a glimpse of him. I think that it is also true that our love, hospitality and acceptance of others can be the occasion for them to perceive that he is touching their lives too.

Furthermore, for the two disciples, recognition finally takes place at table in the breaking of bread, and the larger group seem to be dining, too, when Jesus appears to them. Luke is reminding us that it is in the Eucharist that the presence of the risen Lord continues in the Christian community; in the eucharistic celebration, he can be encountered most powerfully in our midst.[57] Like those original disciples, we celebrate the Eucharist repeatedly as fragile and imperfect people. Eucharist is a reconciling event. It is an encounter with the risen Jesus which has the potential to transform and reshape our lives.[58]

Finally, like the women from the tomb, the two disciples are on fire to share their Good News, reaching out in mission to the others. And the following episode highlights this element, as Jesus sends them out, "preaching repentance for the forgiveness of sins to all nations." Failed disciples have been forgiven and restored; they have experienced the compassionate mercy of God; they can vouch for the truth of the message that they proclaim. This surely gives us courage as we reach out to others in mission and ministry.

Thinking of mission, we can, I believe, find in these narratives an exciting model for our ministry, as we journey with people entrusted to our care. We are called to walk alongside them, even when they are travelling in the wrong direction! We are to be present with them, accepting them where they are, listening to their story, feeling their hopes and their disappointments. We move at their pace, respecting their dignity and freedom. There is a time to ask a question, a time to suggest an explanation, a time to offer a challenge, a time to share our experience too. We can accept and offer hospitality, and share 'table fellowship'. We may break together the bread of Word and Sacrament, and forge together new ways of responding to the Gospel of Jesus.

I am convinced that we all have what can be called 'Emmaus moments'. Perhaps they are not quite so dramatic as in the story we have been pondering, but they are no less real and transforming. If we reflected a little more, we would, I am sure, discover that the texture of our lives is shot through with rays of resurrection light, moments and events that help us to understand a little more what is meant by the Easter proclamation 'He is risen', and the promise this holds for us. There can be situations and settings in our lives where somehow God's presence gently or dramatically breaks through, revealing a deeper dimension embedded in the ordinary and the normal. For some people, music, art, poetry, water, the stars, the kitchen table, the look in a friend's eyes, the smile on a child's face … can carry transforming power. For others, peace after conflict, calm after storm, fresh stream water on aching feet, the snowdrops and daffodils of spring after long, grey winters, can be moments of revelation. For some, the epiphany moment may be recovery from serious illness, success after failure and disappointment, reunion after separation or estrangement, relief from tension, anxiety or depression, liberation from any form of darkness … in short, any death situation transformed into a situation of newness, life and promise. For the followers of Jesus, the ordinary is far from ordinary; there is always a transcendent dimension; God is always with us; for "in Him we live and move and have our being" (Acts 17:28).

Notes

1   Luke's name has been attached to the Third Gospel since the late second century. Consensus suggests that he wrote his Gospel during the years 80–90 CE, for a mainly Gentile audience, be that his own urban community or other church communities in areas of Greece with direct or indirect links to the earlier Pauline mission. Luke is also responsible for the book of Acts, composed as a complementary volume and devoted to the growth of the early Church. A second or third generation Christian (1:1–3), he was not an eyewitness to the life of Jesus, but depends on Mark, 'Q' and other oral and written traditions, which scholars refer to as 'L'.

2   This chapter is a slightly updated version of chapter 14 in my *Walking with Luke* (Bolton: Don Bosco Publications, 2017).

3   Brown, *Risen Christ*, 41, notes that in the Infancy Narrative, Luke stresses how those involved observed the Law (1:6, 8–9; 2:21–25, 37, 39, 41–42). This is again the case here.

4   Some manuscripts say, "the body of the Lord Jesus". Luke T. Johnson, *The Gospel of Luke* (Collegeville, MN, Liturgical Press, 1991), 386, considers it original (see 10:1; 11:39); Luke uses it in Acts 1:21; 2:36; 4:33; 8:16; also I. Howard Marshall, *The Gospel of Luke* (Exeter: Paternoster Press, 1978), 884. John T. Carroll, *Luke: A*

Commentary (Louisville: Westminster John Knox Press, 2012), 476, n. (a), concludes that it is congruent with what is found elsewhere in the narrative. Joel B. Green, *The Gospel of Luke*, NICNT (Cambridge: Eerdmans, 1997), 837, notes that the identity and status of Jesus before God have not in any way been negated or diminished by his shameful rejection and ignominious execution. Carroll, *Luke*, 476, notes the double use of "found" (*heuron*); also, Christopher F. Evans, *Saint Luke* (London: SCM, 1990), 893; Green, *Luke*, 837.

5   They are later identified as angels (24:23), as their garb implies. They function as interpreters like the angels who visit the shepherds in the Infancy Narrative. Denis McBride, *The Gospel of Luke* (Dublin: Dominican Publications, 1991), 314; George B. Caird, *St. Luke* (London: Pelican, 1963), 256; Carroll, *Luke*, 476–77; Johnson, *Luke*, 387; Marshall, *Luke*, 885, and Robert C. Tannehill, *Luke* (Nashville: Abingdon Press, 1996), 349, see them as parallel to the two heavenly witnesses at the transfiguration (9:29), who spoke to Jesus concerning his "exodus" in Jerusalem. Tannehill, *Luke*, 349, comments that the preference for two may stem from the idea that two provide a more reliable witness than one (see Deut 19:15). Eugene LaVerdiere, *Luke* (Dublin: Veritas, 1980), 281, notes other pairings (10:1; 19:29–35; 22:7–13; 24:13–35).

6   Evans, *Luke*, 895; Marshall, *Luke*, 885, suggests an attempt to avoid the bright light. Brown, *Risen Christ*, 42, recalls the shepherds in the Infancy Narrative (2:9–10).

7   The 'divine passive' in Greek (ēgerthē) indicates the agency of God. Some early manuscripts omit this phrase, but it is nowadays judged to belong to the original Lukan text. See Moloney, *Resurrection*, 95, n. 43. The phrase echoes 20:38, Jesus' reply to the Sadducees: "he is God not of the dead but of the living." Brown, *Risen Christ*, 42, notes that the women can see that Jesus is not there, but that the reason for this is resurrection they must take on faith.

8   See 9:22, 44; 18:32–33. Those responsible for Jesus' arrest and death are here referred to as "sinners", rather than "the elders, chief priests and scribes" of 9:22. "Crucified" is used here rather than "killed", and a different verb for "rise". Luke uses "must" (*dei*) forty-one times. In Mark the young man/angel announces that Jesus will go before the disciples to Galilee (16:7; 14:28). Luke changes this message, referring instead to what Jesus has already said while in Galilee. Fuller, *Resurrection Narratives*, 97, states that his changes are clearly motivated by his editorial requirements; he intends to record the appearances of the risen Jesus in Jerusalem, not Galilee. During his appearances at Emmaus and in the Jerusalem room, Jesus reiterates the necessity of the death/resurrection pattern, and its links with scripture (24: 26, 44, 46). His earlier words, now remembered, are fulfilled; later in the chapter it is the words of scripture which are said to be fulfilled. Dunn, *Jesus Remembered*, 830, n. 17, notes that it is hardly possible to evade the conclusion that Luke has modified Mark; he has chosen to omit any reference to or account of resurrection appearances in Galilee. Carroll, *Luke*, 478, refers to the literary style of repetition-with-variation; similarly, Green, *Luke*, 832, n. 3.

63

9   Tannehill, *Luke*, 349; Johnson, *Luke*, 387; Evans, *Luke*, 895; Green, *Luke*, 837-38; Brown, *Risen Christ*, 42. Carroll, *Luke*, 477, refers to a rekindling of forgotten or suppressed memory. Moloney, *Resurrection*, 95, n. 44, notes that "remembering" is an important Lukan theme, part of his presentation of Jesus as a prophet whose words and actions are remembered.

10   Green, *Luke*, 838. Jesus' prophecy is the content of the memory, as with Peter in 22:61. Moloney, *Resurrection*, 80, states that "the women must be regarded as coming to Easter faith" through their remembering.

11   Evans, *Luke*, 897, understands the "others", Galilean disciples, as the nucleus of the future Church along with the eleven. On p. 898, he suggests that mention of additional women present may be to increase the weight of female testimony.

12   Mary Magdalene and Joanna were named in 8:2-3, along with Salome, who is not mentioned here, but is named in Mark 16:1. The other Mary is also found in Mark 16:1. Mark's three lists are not entirely consistent. In Luke 8:2 it is stated that seven demons had gone out of Mary Magdalene; Joanna was said to be the wife of Herod's steward Chuza.

13   McBride, *Luke*, 315. Tannehill, *Luke*, 351, notes cultural resistance to women as witnesses; Moloney, *Resurrection*, 81, refers to the disciples being caught in cultural prejudices. Johnson, *Luke*, 388, believes the term "could scarcely be more condescending," communicating "an air of male superiority." Green, *Luke*, 839, notes that technically the term refers to the delirium caused by high fever, but it is also used in sarcastic conversation. On p. 839-40 he notes that the dismissive response of the male disciples to the message and its significance is better explained with reference to the fact that those doing the reporting are women in a world biased against the admissibility of women as witnesses. N. Tom Wright, *Luke for Everyone* (London: SPCK, 2001), 290, suggests "crazy with grief and lack of sleep."

14   A visit by some of the disciples, without specific indication that Peter was among them, is mentioned in the later Emmaus narrative (24:24). This item (v. 12) is missing from the Western manuscript tradition. Some consider it a scribal addition based on John 20: 6-7. Tannehill, *Luke*, 351, maintains that recent scholarship tends to favour inclusion; also, Johnson, *Luke*, 388; Moloney, *Resurrection*, 95, n. 48; Joseph A. Fitzmyer, *The Gospel according to Luke*, 2 vols. (New York: Doubleday, 1981, 1985), 2, 1542, 1547; Green, *Luke*, 840, n. 17; LaVerdiere, *Luke*, 282. Carroll, *Luke*, 479, is of the opinion that the earliest version of Luke did not contain verse 12, which is an interpolation; similarly, Evans, *Luke*, 900. Mention of Peter here helps bridge the gap between the prayer of Jesus that Peter will turn and strengthen his brothers, and his later role in Acts. Green, *Luke*, 836, writes that Peter's behaviour portends at least the possibility of a more mature understanding of Jesus' message by the disciples.

15   Fuller, *Resurrection Narratives*, 104. Evans, *Luke*, 901, recognises its dramatic quality and its artistry. Perrin, *Resurrection*, 65, writes that it "represents the consummate literary art of the evangelist Luke at its best." Fitzmyer, *Luke*, 2, 1554–55, believes that there is a tradition behind the story (like Mark 16:12–13) upon which Luke has freely built; indications include Emmaus, Cleopas, and the kerygma of v. 34. Brown, *Risen Christ*, 45, n. 53, notes the view that Luke has dramatised a pre-Gospel tradition (like that in Mark 16:12–13). Fuller, *Resurrection Narratives*, 106, provides a possible early form, which may stem from the Syrian community. Dunn, *Jesus Remembered*, 847–48, observes that the marks of Luke's style and skill as a storyteller are evident. Characteristic themes are: Jesus as a prophet, the attributing of his crucifixion directly to the Jewish leadership, scripture proving that the Messiah should suffer, the climax of the breaking of bread. There are also signs of an older tradition: the naming of Cleopas and Emmaus, their expectations concerning Jesus, the note that some male disciples visited the tomb. He notes the view of Fitzmyer (*Luke*, 2, 1554–55), that Mark 16:12–13, is a snippet of pre-Lukan tradition, which Luke built up into his dramatic story, rather than a late summary of the Lukan account. He believes, p. 849, that Luke took up the basic tradition simply because it was there.

16   Carroll, *Luke*, 480.

17   Carroll, *Luke*, 482, observes that in rejoining his followers the risen Lord resumes his teaching role, feasts with them at table and interprets the recent hope-deflating events in the light of the Jewish scriptures.

18   Chapter 2, n. 32. Green, *Luke*, 842, suggests a structure involving inverted parallelism, and Carroll, *Luke*, 482, a concentric structure.

19   For details of possibilities, see Marshall, *Luke*, 892–93; he concludes that certainty is impossible. Fitzmyer, *Luke*, 2, 1562, observes that what matters for Luke is the place's proximity to Jerusalem; likewise, Johnson, *Luke*, 393. Moloney, *Resurrection*, 96, lists several authors who miss the importance of the fact that they are walking *away* from Jerusalem. Carroll, *Luke*, 483, notes that the village is near Jerusalem but not Jerusalem itself; the spatial movement away from the city bears symbolic meaning.

20   Caird, *Luke*, 259; McBride, *Luke*, 317. Fitzmyer, *Luke*, 2, 1561, suggests that the unnamed disciple may be one of the eleven; on 2, 1563, he dismisses any link between Cleopas (Cleopatros) and Clopas. However, Fuller, *Resurrection Narratives*, 107, notes that Jews often took a similar sounding Greek name in addition to their Semitic name. On p. 108 he lists several names which have been proposed; similarly, Marshall, *Luke*, 894. Schneiders, *Jesus Risen*, 11, comments "perhaps the wife of Clopas".

21   Francis J. Moloney, *Reading the New Testament in the Church* (Grand Rapids, MI: Baker Academic, 2015), 129; *Resurrection*, 81–82, they have made the wrong choice, abandoning God's saving story; McBride, *Luke*, 316.

22   Carroll, *Luke*, 483, notes the use of two verbs *homilein* and *syzētein*, suggesting a spirited exchange of differing opinions.

23   Here the verb is *antiballō*, which means to toss back and forth.

24   The Greek is *paroikein*. Johnson, *Luke*, 393, notes that the term is appropriate for someone staying in the city for the festival. Brendan Byrne, *The Hospitality of God* (Collegeville, MN: Liturgical Press, 2000), 187, considers the question sharp, cynical and ironic.

25   Moloney, *Resurrection*, 82, believes that the use of the divine passive indicates the action of God here. In *Reading*, 129, he comments that although God is not mentioned, God is responsible; God is not abandoning the disciples; likewise, Byrne, *Hospitality*, 187. Carroll, *Luke*, 483, refers to God's agency in the concealment and disclosure alike. Caird, *Luke*, 257, writes: "In retrospect their failure to recognise him seemed so odd that they could only suppose a supernatural restraint had been imposed on their vision and not removed until their minds were prepared for the staggering revelation" to come. Green, *Luke*, 845, disagrees with this view. Fitzmyer, *Luke*, 2, 1558, sees it as a literary device to advance the story and create suspense. They need to be instructed first. Evans, *Luke*, 905, holds that probably a supernatural action of God is denoted; this he sees as a theological narrative device.

26   Moloney, *Resurrection*, 96, n. 52, quotes with approval Tannehill's view that they are not without guilt in their inability to recognise Jesus. They are not ready to deal with Jesus' death, and this is a culpable failure. Johnson, *Luke*, 395, translates "reluctant to believe", implying moral failure.

27   Jesus is treated as an uninformed stranger yet is the subject of all that has happened.

28   Moloney, *Reading*, 130, calls this "a catechetical-liturgical process."

29   Jesus refers to himself as a prophet in 4:24 and 13:33, both linked with rejection and death. In Acts, he is put forward as the expected prophet like Moses (3:22; 7:37), an alternative eschatological expectation. See Tannehill, *Luke*, 353; on p. 356, he writes that scripture and the story of Jesus are being read in the light of a presumed prophetic destiny that includes suffering, rejection and even death.

30   Fitzmyer, *Luke*, 2, 1564, notes that the Jewish authorities are held responsible, not the Romans (see 23:13). Again, Luke substitutes "crucified" for "put to death". Brown, *Risen Christ*, 46, n. 55, believes that this refutes the claim, based on there being no formal condemnation in the Jewish trial, that Luke did not blame the Jewish authorities for the death of Jesus.

31   Moses is described like this in Acts 7:22; see also Deut 34:10–12. See Green, *Luke*, 846; Fuller, *Resurrection Narratives*, 110. There is an echo of Anna's words in 2:38. Their expectations of national deliverance were misguided.

32   In Luke's empty tomb story Peter went to the tomb alone.

33   Moloney, *Resurrection*, 83; *Reading*, 130. They have not remembered his words. Green, *Luke*, 848, notes the importance of "seeing" for Luke. Carroll, *Luke*, 484, too observes that the disciples cannot see; visual perception is a metaphor for understanding.

34   Carroll, *Luke*, 484, n. 11: "heart" in both cognitive and affective dimensions, as the locus of thinking, attitude and life-orienting commitment.

35   Caird, *Luke*, 258. For Johnson, *Luke*, 396, "glory" means kingly rule and authority; similarly, Tannehill, *Luke*, 355. Evans, *Luke*, 910, understands "glory" as a heavenly mode of existence connected with the resurrection. Moloney, *Resurrection*, 84, calls this a liturgy of the Word. He notes the use of the passive to indicate Jesus' role in responding to God's design, and the mention of fulfilment and necessity (*dei*). No specific references are provided by the evangelist. For Fuller, *Resurrection Narratives*, 111, the fulfilment of scripture is the principal motif of the story. It is also part of the primitive formula in 1 Cor 15:3–4. Brown, *Risen Christ*, 48, refers to the Christian preaching in Acts 3:18; 17:3; 26:23 concerning the theme of the Messiah who must first suffer, which was not an expectation in pre-Christian Judaism. In n. 58 he observes that although some arguments based on scripture developed in debates with non-believing Jews, the primary goal was to provide understanding for believers.

36   The Greek is *prospoieō*, meaning to pretend, to act as though.

37   The verb *parabiazō* means to force or urge; it denotes compulsion.

38   Fitzmyer, *Luke*, 2, 1567, points out that according to Jewish reckoning the Sunday is over; Luke seems to consider the time after sundown to be the same day.

39   R. J. Karris, 'God's Boundary-Breaking Mercy', *The Bible Today* 24 (1986), 27–28.

40   Green, *Luke*, 849, links the gesture with 9:16, the miraculous feeding. Fitzmyer, *Luke*, 2, 1568, recalls also 22:19, the multiplication and the Supper; also, Marshall, *Luke*, 898. Fitzmyer, *Luke*, 2, 1559, states that the action of Jesus recalls the Supper, and becomes the classic Lukan way of referring to the Eucharist. Moloney, *Reading*, 131, writes: "The memory of the many meals that Jesus has shared with them, and especially the meal he shared on the night before he died, opens their eyes and anticipates the many meals that will be celebrated in the future"; also, *Resurrection*, 84–85; similarly, Johnson, *Luke*, 396. Caird, *Luke*, 259, refers to other meals that Jesus had held with his friends, perhaps, like the Last Supper, as anticipations of the messianic banquet of the Kingdom. Breaking bread is a Lukan expression (Acts 2:42, 46; 20:7, 11; 27:35).

41   McBride, *Luke*, 320. Johnson, *Luke*, 397, notes that the same verb is used both for opening the scriptures and the opening of their eyes. "As they perceived the true, messianic meaning of the Scripture, they were also able to 'see' Jesus in the breaking of the bread." Also, Tannehill, *Luke*, 358; Evans, *Luke*, 914.

42   Moloney, *Resurrection,* 85. He notes that the name Simon is used here, as at his original call (4:38), and in foretelling the denials (22:31). He, too, is a failed disciple, a sinner who has been forgiven. Luke states the appearance to Peter, as does Paul in 1 Cor 15:5; there is no narrative. Brown, *Risen Christ,* 51, comments that apostolic faith is not based on the empty tomb story or even a message of angels, but on an actual encounter with Jesus.

43   Johnson, *Luke,* 398, sees the Emmaus story as providing an emotionally satisfying bridge between the shock of absence and the shock of full presence. Dunn, *Jesus Remembered,* 849–50, sees a common core in the Jerusalem stories of Luke and John, elaborated by each evangelist in their typical ways. We have two well developed versions and one creedal formula of a tradition which was probably told and retold in the early Christian communities. In n. 107, he suggests that it is more plausible that that the *initial* talk of a group experience among those who participated in it took a *narrative* form rather than a confessional, kerygmatic one. Some manuscripts omit the greeting; Carroll, *Luke,* 489, 490, considers it an interpolation by a scribe wishing to conform Luke with John (20:19, 26). Dunn, *Jesus Remembered,* 849, n.98, maintains that the majority opinion now concludes that these verses (24: 36b, 40) were part of Luke's original text. As Tannehill, *Luke,* 359, points out, mention of "peace" recalls 1:79; 2:14, 29; 10:5–6; 19:42; it is more than a conventional greeting. For Green, *Luke,* 854, peace for Luke means salvation. Carroll, *Luke,* 488, 491, notes the repetition of the pattern of divine activity through Jesus' revelatory presence and teaching, in overcoming obstacles to the disciples' understanding and secure faith. Francis J. Moloney, *A Body Broken for a Broken People. Marriage, Divorce, and the Eucharist* (Mulgrave: Garratt, 2015), 151; *Resurrection, 87,* lists the many parallels between the Emmaus story and the room scene: they are talking to one another; Jesus appears; he is not recognised; he asks a rhetorical question; there is scripture-based instruction; there are revealing actions with bread and fish; Jesus disappears; they return to Jerusalem. Brown, *Risen Christ,* 51, n. 59, notes the formidable chronological difficulties with the overly long first day of the week, even if Luke is no longer employing a Jewish way of reckoning; see also *Bodily Resurrection,* 102–105.

44   Carroll, *Luke,* 490, refers to "emotional turmoil and cognitive confusion".

45   This is also the case in John 20:19–29, which contains explicit mention of the nail marks. The emphasis in Luke is on Jesus' physical reality. In all appearance stories, Jesus is the same person, but different. There is continuity but transformation. Paul (1 Cor 15:43–49) gives greater emphasis to the transformation; Luke and John perhaps overemphasise the physicality. Caird, *Luke,* 260–61, notes that for Jews, reality was always particular and concrete; it was inevitable that this concreteness should find expression in materialistic imagery. Benedict XVI, *Jesus of Nazareth,* 2, 269, refers to Luke exaggerating in his apostolic zeal. Perrin, *Resurrection,* 69, suggests that this aspect of the story is intended to resist the Hellenistic view that religious heroes overcame death by being transformed into a spiritual being with no contact with the world of flesh. Jesus is not a disembodied spiritual being.

68

46   McBride, *Luke,* 322; Green, *Luke,* 855, who also notes that incontrovertible evidence of Jesus' embodied existence is not capable of producing faith; scriptural illumination is required.

47   Moloney, *Resurrection,* 87, notes that the meal table is the place where he gives them his final instructions. The incident recalls the meal of 9:16. This and the Emmaus meal bring the many Gospel meals to a climax. Byrne, *Hospitality,* 191, also emphasises the meal context; also, Tannehill, *Luke,* 360. Green, *Luke,* 855, n. 9, believes that this should not be read into the text; Evans, *Luke,* 920, maintains that this is not a meal. Carroll, *Luke,* 492, sees Jesus as guest and recipient of the disciples' hospitality; in the future they will be the providers of hospitality.

48   Carroll, *Luke,* 492, notes how the psalms (added here to Law and Prophets) feature prominently in the Christological exegesis of scripture, especially in the speeches of Acts (2:25–28; 4:25–28; 13:33–37). Green, *Luke,* 856, adds that they play an important role in Luke's interpretation of the passion. He also stresses divine purpose and fulfilment.

49   Green, *Luke,* 857–58, notes the importance of Isa 49:6 for Luke (2:32; Acts 13:47). Instead of a centripetal orientation for the universal mission, it is now centrifugal. "Already the effects of the rending of the temple veil at Jesus' death are being felt." "Repentance" means the realignment of one's life (dispositions and behaviours) towards God's purpose. In Acts, the name of Jesus is an important motif. Brown, *Risen Christ,* 55, emphasises that Luke brings the commission under the same scriptural imperative as the passion and resurrection.

50   Moloney, *Resurrection,* 88, observes that it is on the basis of their own experience of repentance and forgiveness that they are commissioned to bear witness to the nations. They are well qualified to do so. Tannehill, *Luke,* 361, notes that forgiveness was central to the mission of John the Baptist and Jesus; it is in Jesus' name, with his authority, that the message is to be proclaimed to all. Carroll, *Luke,* 492, speaks of Jesus' ministry of "release" (*aphesis*), (1:77; 3:3; 4:18–19). Brown, *Risen Christ,* 55, suggests that the proclamation of repentance and forgiveness "in Jesus' name" suggests that both preaching and baptising are envisaged as part of the commission (see Acts 8:12).

51   Johnson, *Luke,* 403, suggests that this promise recalls that of 1:35 to Mary. On p. 406, he points out that in the cases of both Moses and Elijah their spirit was transmitted to their successors at their departure (Deut 34:9; 2 Kgs 2:9). Green, *Luke,* 853, reminds us that the ministry of Jesus has been conducted in the power of the Spirit. Evans, *Luke,* 925–26, sees the exalted Jesus as the dispenser of the Spirit from heaven.

52   Green, *Luke,* 859, notes that this passage contains many textual problems; the NRSV text represents current scholarly consensus. Carroll, *Luke,* 495, states that Bethany recalls the beginning of Jesus' triumphal entry into Jerusalem. The event now underway is a triumphal exit. Green, *Luke,* 860, observes that whereas Luke

has hitherto marked chronology carefully and explicitly, he does not do so here. The impression is that the ascension too took place on the Sunday evening, but Luke leaves open other possibilities, which he exploits in Acts 1:1–11. The group present here is wider than the apostles. In Acts 1:12–15 those present number 120 persons.

53   See 2 Kgs 2:1–18 concerning Elijah and Elisha. Johnson, *Luke*, 403–404, recalls the blessings by Moses (Exod 17:11 LXX; Num 20:11; Exod 39:43) and Aaron (Lev 9:22); Carroll, *Luke*, 495, suggests Moses (Deut 33) and Jacob (Gen 49:28). Some scholars (like McBride, *Luke*, 323; Brown, *Risen Christ*, 57, and Evans, *Luke*, 928) refer to Lev 9:22 and Sir 50:20–22, which suggest reference to a priestly Jesus, operating outside the temple and city. But Luke has so far shown no interest in this idea. The leave-taking of Moses and Abraham is a more likely model. Carroll, *Luke*, 496, notes that after "he withdrew from them", not all manuscripts add "and was carried up into heaven"; he believes that this is a later addition, though this is not certain. For most readers, the ascension imagery completes the story, as Jesus is vindicated by God and is exalted to God's right hand as Messiah and Lord. Marshall, *Luke*, 909, considers evidence for omission to be weak. Perrin, *Resurrection Narratives*, 74, notes that Luke seems to be the first Christian writer to understand the ascension as an event distinct from the resurrection itself.

54   Green, *Luke*, 861, understands this as a visible and concrete way of expressing the elevated status of Jesus, his glory and regal power. His way of suffering and humiliation is embraced by God. The ascension is a prelude to the outpouring of the Spirit and consequent mission of the Church.

55   There is an alternative and longer version of the Ascension in Acts 1:1–11. Johnson, *Luke*, 404, comments that ancient historians were less fastidious in such matters of overlap than are some contemporary scholars. See Byrne, *Hospitality*, 192.

56   Green, *Luke*, 843, notes the themes of journey, hospitality/table fellowship, and scriptural fulfilment. Fitzmyer, *Luke*, 2, 1557–59, lists geographical, revelatory, Christological (as fulfilling Old Testament prophecy), eucharistic.

57   Perrin, *Resurrection*, 68, writes "Luke is telling his readers that the risen Lord can be known to them, as he became known to the two disciples, in the eucharist."

58   Fitzmyer, *Luke*, 2, 1569, acknowledges a eucharistic reference in "the breaking of bread". Carroll, *Luke*, 487, sees the Emmaus meal as a proleptic anticipation of the bread-breaking meals of the community in Acts, and of the eschatological banquet.

Chapter Four
The Resurrection in John 20

The Fourth Evangelist's presentation of the resurrection of Jesus is extremely rich from both theological and spirituality perspectives. Some scholars have maintained that there is no need for resurrection narratives in John; all has been fulfilled on Calvary; Jesus is glorified and does not need divine vindication.[1] It is, indeed, true that the Synoptic slant on the resurrection as God's vindication of Jesus is not a feature of the Johannine text. However, in this Gospel glorification and resurrection stand together as two related though different dimensions of the paschal mystery and Jesus' post-paschal life. The first refers to Jesus' passage from this world to the Father, the second his promised return to his own (14:28).[2]

During the ministry, Jesus three times spoke of his being "lifted up", a term which has two meanings: his being crucified and his being glorified (3:14–15; 8:28; 12:32). Both meanings reach fulfilment on Calvary's hill. Jesus' final words from the cross are "it is finished", mission accomplished (19:30). At the Supper he had prayed to the Father: "I glorified you on earth by finishing the work which you gave me to do (17:4)." In the "hour" Jesus reveals to the world the amazing love of the Father who sent him (3:16–17); in this the Father is glorified. He also reveals the depth of his own love for his sheep, love to the end and the utmost (13:1; 15:12–13). As C.K. Barrett succinctly puts it: "the revelation and the deed of love were complete."[3] Through his being "lifted up", Jesus returns to the Father and is glorified, exalted; his earthly story has reached closure. But the evangelist from the first pages of his Gospel and throughout his narrative has also told of his disciples, following their struggles to understand Jesus, their hesitant journey into faith, a journey by no means accomplished yet. Several times during the Supper Jesus referred to his going away and returning (14:3, 19, 28; 16:16). Resurrection refers to that return.[4] The appearances of the risen Jesus, which we are about to ponder in this chapter, "are not primarily about *Jesus'* post-death experience but about his *disciples'* experience of his return to them."[5] John wishes to explore the meaning and implications of Jesus' resurrection for his community and all who come to believe in Jesus.

The text comprises of four scenes and a concluding statement, which together form a narrative and dramatic unity. The first two scenes take place in a garden around the tomb (1–18): there are two visits to the tomb, by Magdalene, and then by Peter and the Beloved Disciple (1–10); and then the appearance of the risen One to Magdalene occurs (11–18). The subsequent two scenes occur in a Jerusalem room (19–29): Jesus appears to the group of disciples minus Thomas (19–23); he again appears a week later when Thomas is present (24–29).[6] The evangelist is doubtless using old traditions, but he has refashioned them to bring out his own understanding of it all, and the different episodes form a carefully crafted literary whole.[7] Whatever the earlier traditions may have been, in this study we are concerned with the current text as it stands.[8]

The Garden Tomb

Early on the first day of the week, while it was still dark, Mary Magdalene came to the tomb and saw that the stone had been removed from the tomb. So she ran and went to Simon Peter and the other disciple, the one whom Jesus loved, and said to them, "They have taken the Lord out of the tomb, and we do not know where they have laid him." Then Peter and the other disciple set out and went towards the tomb. The two were running together, but the other disciple outran Peter and reached the tomb first. He bent down to look in and saw the linen wrappings lying there, but he did not go in. Then Simon Peter came, following him, and went into the tomb. He saw the linen wrappings lying there, and the cloth that had been on Jesus' head, not lying with the linen wrappings but rolled up in a place by itself. Then the other disciple, who reached the tomb first, also went in, and he saw and believed; for as yet they did not understand the scripture, that he must rise from the dead. Then the disciples returned to their homes.

The setting is the garden in which Jesus was buried in a new tomb by Joseph of Arimathea and Nicodemus with lavish style worthy of a king.[9] Their action, in emerging from the shadows into the open, is an indication of the beginning (the "gathering") of the new community, now that the "hour" has come and Jesus has been "lifted up". In John's burial account there is no mention of the stone being rolled across the tomb's entrance, nor of the presence of the women, silently watching, but these traditional details are presupposed.

It is the first day of the week, a comment which perhaps suggests the start of something new.[10] It is early in the morning and still dark. The engulfing darkness mirrors Mary's inner disposition as she makes the journey to the tomb, grieving and devoid of hope. She is alone. The purpose of her visit is not specified. She probably comes with aching heart to mourn her beloved Jesus, overcome by the brutal and ultimate reality of death. She is caught up with mortality.[11] To her horror she sees that the stone has been rolled away from the entrance, and she assumes that the tomb is empty. Her initial distress intensified, she rushes off to find the two leading disciples of Jesus, Simon Peter and the enigmatic disciple whom Jesus loved,[12] and tells them the dreadful news: "They have taken the Lord out of the tomb, and we do not know where they have laid him."[13] She jumps to the conclusion that the body of Jesus has been stolen.[14] Grave robbery was not uncommon; people sometimes sought valuables in the tomb, and there was the possibility of hate crime.[15] She does not intuit God's action or imagine the possibility of resurrection.[16]

Peter and the "other disciple" run to the tomb to see for themselves.[17] The other disciple reaches the tomb first. He bends down and through the low opening is able to see the linen cloths lying on the ground, but deferentially he waits until Simon Peter arrives. This is a literary delaying tactic.[18] Peter rushes in and sees the cloths (*othonia*) and also the head napkin or veil (*soudarion*), folded and left separately on one side.[19] The other disciple then follows him into the tomb. He is able to decode the message conveyed by the empty tomb and the cloths, especially the folded veil, which he was unable to see before, and perceives the action of God in this place.[20] He "saw and believed", we are told, and then the two depart, leaving the tomb and the garden.[21] The narrator comments that "as yet they did not know the scripture, that he must rise from the dead."[22]

It would seem that Mary accompanied them back to the tomb or followed closely behind. When they leave for their homes, Simon Peter still unbelieving, and the Beloved Disciple taciturn in his belief, she remains, now centre stage, standing near the tomb in considerable distress.[23] The scene is set for a remarkable encounter.[24]

> But Mary stood weeping outside the tomb. As she wept, she bent over to look into the tomb; and she saw two angels in white, sitting where the body of Jesus had been lying, one at the head and the other at the feet. They said to her,

"Woman, why are you weeping?" She said to them, "They have taken away my Lord, and I do not know where they have laid him." When she had said this, she turned around and saw Jesus standing there, but she did not know that it was Jesus. Jesus said to her, "Woman, why are you weeping? Whom are you looking for?" Supposing him to be the gardener, she said to him, "Sir, if you have carried him away, tell me where you have laid him, and I will take him away." Jesus said to her, "Mary!" She turned and said to him in Hebrew, "Rabbouni!" (which means Teacher). Jesus said to her, "Do not hold on to me, because I have not yet ascended to the Father. But go to my brothers and say to them, 'I am ascending to my Father and your Father, to my God and your God'." Mary Magdalene went and announced to the disciples, "I have seen the Lord"; and she told them that he had said these things to her.

The resurrection narratives in the different Gospels follow the same basic literary pattern that contains five constituent elements, as we have seen: an initial situation of loss, the unexpected presence of the risen Jesus, doubt or failure to recognise him, recognition, commissioning. This is a useful working framework, and the current story fits the pattern very well. For the episode which we are considering, Sandra Schneiders proposes three different elements: weeping, turning and announcing, and, with a slight variation, I shall here follow this structure. [25]

The bereavement, grief, weeping element is clearly a key feature of the early part of the story, reflecting Mary's intense sense of loss.[26] "Her weeping suggests frustration as well as grief."[27] There is a persistent emphasis on emptiness and absence. Twice Mary is asked the reason for her weeping; first by the two angelic figures seated at either end of the burial shelf, secondly by the gardener. Her reply to the angels, who are signs that God has been at work, echoes her earlier words to the disciples, except that she speaks in the singular rather than the plural, which highlights her personal relationship, perhaps suggesting a little possessiveness.[28] She is oblivious to the significance of their presence;[29] she clearly does not suspect that Jesus has been raised.[30]

However, rather than weeping, I personally prefer to see the structural issue as one of searching or seeking. Searching is a more dynamic term; it moves the narrative forward; there are also echoes of the Song of Songs, the search of the lover for her beloved (3:1–4). Mary peers into the tomb. Later the "gardener" asks her: "Who are you looking for?", a question which recalls that posed by Jesus to his earliest disciples.[31] And this highlights the reason why she is weeping. Mary of Magdala has found love and meaning in Jesus, as is evident from her presence at the cross and her solitary journey to the tomb in the dark. And now Jesus has been taken away, not only personally in death, but his corpse as well. She searches for him desperately with grim determination. She will not abandon her search. Her plea to the gardener is wrung from one clutching at straws:[32] "Sir, if you have carried him away, tell me where you have laid him, and I will take him away." (20:15) But she is searching for the wrong thing, a dead body, and she is searching in the wrong place. And when the real object of her search arrives on the scene, Mary, blinded by her tears and preoccupied about grave robbers, fails to recognise him, mistaking him for the gardener. The irony is intense. She remains in unbelief and confusion, obsessively fixated on the physical presence of the earthly Jesus.

Twice the evangelist mentions Mary's turning. After the angels have addressed her, at which she is not startled or filled with fear, which is the usual biblical response, she turns away from this sign of God's action in the tomb and turns back to her quest for a dead body and the past with which it is associated.[33] It is then that she comes face to face with the gardener. The risen Jesus then speaks her name, "Mary!" The power of a name! The surprise of a voice no longer silent! Here the Good Shepherd is calling his sheep by name, and she recognises his voice.[34] It is such a magical, numinous moment, the moment of recognition, the moment of transformation. The text states that at that point she "turned", a gesture symbolising the inner change which is taking place, her movement into faith. Instead of the corpse she was seeking, there stands before her a real, living person, her Jesus, her Lord. "Rabbuni! My Teacher!" she cries in joyful response, with deep respect, great spontaneity and transparent affection. She wants to hold on to this moment forever and never let Jesus go, for he is her meaning, it is he who enables her to discover her true self, he is her love and her life, and she has found again the one she sought.[35]

But no, Jesus has not returned as he was before. The old familiar name does not capture his true identity.[36] The old way of relating cannot be resumed. This is not the Jesus of the past. Mary's physical touching, clinging, holding on to him, natural as it is, expresses her misunderstanding of the nature of his presence.[37] Through being "uplifted" Jesus has returned to the Father and is now the glorified risen One. Jesus is truly alive and present, but in a new and vastly different way. A resurrection appearance and permanent presence are different.[38] Mary needs to come to understand this; further growth is required; her faith journey must continue; another threshold remains to be crossed.[39] From the Father's side he will send the Spirit, the Paraclete, bringing his mission to completion. It will be through the Spirit that Jesus will remain and abide with her and his followers on into the future. This Jesus had promised at the Supper. Now she must indeed turn; she must loosen her embrace, let go and move forward into the future, into a new way of being, relating and living.[40]

The final stage of the narrative consists in Mary's commissioning by the risen Jesus: "Go to my brothers and say to them, 'I am ascending to my Father and your Father, to my God and your God'." (20:17) The imperative is strong. Mary has received the revelation of Jesus, and is formally sent on mission, sent as 'the apostle to the apostles', commissioned to bear witness, and to announce the new situation which is unfolding. "The work of the Word made flesh is complete, and its fruits are available to his disciples."[41] The phrasing of the message is carefully balanced (recalling Ruth 1:16 and the covenant formulas of Jeremiah 31:3 and Ezekiel 36:28).[42] It emphasises at the same time the otherness of Jesus and his distinctive relationship to the Father, and also his belonging and closeness to the disciples. As a result of his being "lifted up", his followers are for the first time referred to as his brothers and sisters, able to call his Father their Father.[43] The Father of Jesus now becomes the Father of his disciples; a new relationship with the Father and with Jesus is established. The purpose of his coming in the first place, his being sent, is now fulfilled; they have become children of God (1:13). The risen One draws them into the mystery of the Father's enduring love, the mystery of 'abiding'. Through the event of the "hour" the new covenant community is coming into being, the new family of God, God's household, is coming to birth.

Mary obeys the word of Jesus. She once more leaves the garden tomb, retracing her steps. This time she is not the harbinger of perplexing and disconcerting news about an empty tomb. She has been the first to encounter the risen Lord; she has come to faith through seeing the risen Jesus. The purpose of her journey is to announce to the disciples the Easter kerygma so full of promise: "I have seen the Lord!"[44] The link is again made between seeing and hearing, believing and bearing witness.[45] She is "an official apostolic witness of the resurrection."[46]

Her words will resound beyond that intimate circle, and draw others into the experience, enabling them to find meaning, true selfhood and lasting love in relationship with the risen Jesus. Within the narrative itself, her proclamation and witness to the other disciples sets the stage and prepares the way for the appearance of the risen One in the room where they are fearfully taking refuge, and for the outpouring of the life-giving and transforming Spirit, the gift which brings Jesus' mission to fulfilment.[47] Thus the garden has become the garden of new creation and new covenant; and Magdalene is "the apostolic witness upon whom the paschal faith of the community was founded."[48]

Reflections

Searching

Although this story is about Mary from Magdala, her coming to faith, her foundational apostolic witness, her pivotal role in the early community, it is possible for us today to find ourselves in the narrative. The question of the gardener, really the risen Jesus, is challenging and fundamental: "Who are you looking for?" It echoes a question put by Jesus to the two disciples of John the Baptist who were following him down the path right at the beginning of the story: "What are you looking for?" Who and what indeed are we looking for? Mary, like all of us, had been seeking meaning, friendship, fulfilment, hope, aliveness. She had found them in Jesus. The 'what' was in fact a 'who'. In our case, in our life's search, the 'what' and the 'who' perhaps do not always coincide; they can be prised apart. Like Magdalene in the garden, we can be looking for the wrong thing, looking in the wrong place. We can fail to recognise what we are looking for, even when it is there before our eyes. So many of our contemporaries and young people, sadly, find themselves in this situation.

Our world today is, I feel, increasingly becoming a 'what' world. It is what we have and what we do that matters, that conveys identity, bestows worth. The advertising agencies exploit this so effectively: magnificent houses, shining cars, brilliant technological gadgets, fashionable clothes, exotic holidays, signs of success … And our lives can be dominated by systems, reports, assessments, schedules, targets. In education and the health service and social services in the UK, there is intense pressure towards 'whatification', to coin a term. We can become bogged down in things, in busyness and trivia. As Christians we can quite easily get caught up in this floodtide and lose focus and perspective. As a Church over the centuries we have developed new 'whats', which, I feel, have often blurred our vision of the 'who'.

Our deepest human 'whats', our fundamental thirsts, needs and longings, coalesce into a 'who'. "Who are you looking for?" It is Jesus who alone can satisfy what is at the core of our being, who can set us free and give us life in its fullness. And the 'who' that is Jesus pushes us towards other 'whos': our brothers and sisters, our young people, the people we seek to serve. We must in life and ministry maintain and promote the primacy of the 'who'. It is the people that matter.

Turning

In the journey of Christian discipleship there is the constant element of turning and letting go. We cannot stay as we are, locked into sameness. Like Magdalene we often find that we want things to remain as they were; we find it hard to turn away, let go and move on. The old and the familiar and the tried cast a holding spell on us. Yet Jesus, as he calls our name, frequently asks us to embrace the new, to risk the unknown, to step forward. It is possibly something like a child reluctantly coming forth from the security of the mother's womb into a new world. The child has no idea of the wonders and new possibilities that await it until the birthing process is complete.[49]

"Do not cling." Openness to respond to God's call, obedience for mission, can really hurt. We may have to move geographically, leaving hills, open fields, the singing of early morning birds for the noise and dust and buzz of the city, or vice versa. It may be a question of changing job or responsibility or coming to terms with new organisational changes and personnel in our place of work, or the onset of retirement. It may simply be the need to relinquish pet ideas or preferred ways of doing things, sacred and comfortable routines. It may be shifts in significant relationships. It may be the need to welcome the changes that are part of the ageing process.[50] The following of Jesus demands poverty of spirit and inner freedom, as we prepare for the ultimate letting go. What is true for us as individuals can apply to us as religious, parish communities and apostolic teams too. Becoming fully alive demands the dynamic of turning and letting go.

In turning away, we turn towards, and we encounter Jesus, the risen One. He remains the answer to our quest. It is he who enables us to find our true selfhood as individuals, our true identity as Christian communities. It is he who is the love of our life. It is he who is the centre. It is our relationship with him which colours everything else; the way we see ourselves (our self-image), the way we live our sexuality, our attitude to possessions and status and success, our seeking to discern the demands of love in our lives and ministries, and to respond to those demands. If he isn't there, we are back sitting around a tomb, dreaming of the past, gazing sadly into emptiness.

Announcing

Having been found by Jesus, like Magdalene we are sent on mission. Our experience just has to be shared with others. We are to tell them that God is our loving Father and their loving Father. We are to tell them that "I have seen the Lord." Jesus is risen, is alive, is central to our lives, is present with us; we are his friends, his brothers and sisters. This is our message as we seek to share our 'who'. And how are we going to communicate this gladdening news? We are bearers of his revelation, his life-giving word. Evangelisation, catechesis and technological proficiency are important. I do not underrate these. But we are sent above all to bear witness in our daily living to the reality of the risen Jesus as someone whom we know as saviour and friend. This comes across through the sparkle in our eyes, the warmth of our smile, the genuineness of our welcome, acceptance and hospitality, the song in our heart, the lightness of our step, the gentleness of our compassionate touch. It is communicated through the excitement of our vision, our enthusiasm for what we are engaged in, our freedom and flexibility, the simplicity and generosity of our self-giving and service. Basically, it all has to do with who he is for us and who we are for him. "I have seen the Lord."

As Mary left the garden, walking swiftly into her unexpected future, I imagine that she noticed for the first time that day that the birds were singing, the sun was warm on her back, and a gentle breeze was caressing her hair. A deep peace pervaded her being, and she was aching with joy and love.

Room Appearances

The beautiful narrative of Magdalene's encounter with the risen Jesus is followed by two appearance stories in which the risen One meets the larger group of disciples.[51] These both take place in a room in Jerusalem, the second a week after the first. The basic pattern, which we have seen in the other stories, can readily be detected. However, the element of hesitancy, non-recognition and doubt is omitted in the first appearance and is transferred to the second episode, where it is personified in Thomas.[52]

The First Appearance

> When it was evening on that day, the first day of the week, and the doors of the house where the disciples had met were locked for fear of the Jews, Jesus came and stood among them and said, "Peace be with you." After he said this, he showed them his hands and his side. Then the disciples rejoiced when they saw the Lord. Jesus said to them again, "Peace be with you. As the Father has sent me, so I send you." When he had said this, he breathed on them and said to them, "Receive the Holy Spirit. If you forgive the sins of any, they are forgiven them; if you retain the sins of any, they are retained." (20: 19–23)

It is now the evening of that same day, the first day of the week, the day of the discovery of the empty tomb and Magdalene's encounter with the risen Jesus.[53] In spite of her announcement, presumed but not described, the disciples are locked in the room behind closed doors. Her message seems to have made no impact. The reason for this is immediately made explicit; it is for fear of the "Jews", the religious authorities responsible for Jesus' death.[54] The composition of the group is unclear. Most scholars think that John intends the inner group, including Peter and the Beloved Disciple, as in the wider tradition, but without Judas and Thomas.[55] Suddenly and unexpectedly Jesus comes[56] and stands in their midst.[57] Closed doors in their natural solidity are no barrier for him. He overcomes the limits which normal human circumstances impose and is not deterred by any form of human conditioning. He now belongs to the world "above"; he is present but in a different way from before.[58] He greets them: "Peace be with you". "Peace" was a normal, everyday greeting, a wish for well-being, but here it is more, for in Christian usage it came to acquire deeper meaning.[59] In the Old Testament it often signified that the audience had nothing to fear from the divine manifestation they were witnessing (Judg 6:23; Dan 10:19).[60] Here the greeting fulfils Jesus' Supper promise: "Peace I leave with you; my peace I give to you" (14:27–28; 16:33), when Jesus' peace is linked with his return among them.[61] Jesus' words are not a wish, but a declaration, a statement of fact, a present reality.[62] "He comes into their fear, their shame, their infidelity, their cowardice, not to accuse or retaliate, not to extract a confession or demand reparation, not to do to them what they have done to him. He sets no conditions for their rehabilitation."[63]

He then shows them his hands and his side.[64] This detail emphasises the continuity between the crucified and risen One, the permanent link between these two aspects of Jesus' identity, his self-giving and his exaltation. It is an act of revelation.[65] The disciples recognise him. There is no element of hesitation or doubt or confusion; this will be the theme of the next episode.[66] Their reaction to the sight of Jesus is to be filled with joy; fear has disappeared. Peace and joy are the marks of the eschatological period. Jesus during the Supper said: "A little while, and you will no longer see me, and again a little while and you will see me" (16:16), promising joy at his return: "So you have pain now; but I will see you again, and your hearts will rejoice, and no one will take your joy from you" (16:22; also 15:11; 17:13). Jesus' promise has come true.[67] The use of "Lord" is John's typical post-resurrection title for Jesus, ordinarily used in the community. It implies belief.

Jesus again wishes them "Peace", and then commissions them and sends them forth, in keeping with his Supper prayer (17:18):[68] "As the Father sent me, so am I sending you." The gift of peace takes away fear of others' opinions, hostile attitudes or persecution.[69] The disciples are to be bearers of the fruits of Jesus' victory to the world beyond the time and characters of Jesus' story. The model or pattern for this commissioning is the Father's sending of the Son (see also 17:18). During the ministry there is no mission of the disciples, as in the Synoptic tradition, nor does John refer to them as apostles. He now joins the common resurrection tradition according to which the risen One entrusts a saving mission to those to whom he appeared. John's special theological contribution is the grounding of the mission in the Father's sending the Son, which is a major theme of the Gospel.[70] Their mission is to continue his mission, to be to the world what he has been to the world, revealing God's presence and love and enabling people to become caught up in God's life; this becomes possible only through the gift of the Spirit.[71] In 17:17–19 a relationship is made between the consecration of the disciples in truth and their being sent, again in parallel with Jesus' consecration and being sent, and it is the Spirit who consecrates them.[72] The other evangelists mention a mission to the world or the Gentiles; for John the mission is as wide as the mission of Jesus himself.[73] And "whoever receives the one whom I send receives me; and whoever receives me receives him who sent me" (13:20). "The mission of Jesus is continued in the works of the disciples who share in Jesus' life and abide in his love through the gift of the Holy Spirit."[74]

After his words of commissioning,[75] the risen One then breathes on his disciples, and says: "Receive the Holy Spirit", fulfilling his promise at the Supper (15:26), and the Baptist's earlier identification of Jesus by the Jordan (1:33).[76] There is a link between his words of sending, his breathing action and his accompanying words. This breathing evokes the creation story in Gen 2:7 LXX: "Yahweh God shaped man from the soil of the ground and blew the breath of life into his nostrils, and man became a living being."[77] The imagery of the creative dawn is echoed in Psalm 104:29–30: "Turn away your face and they panic; take back their breath and they die and revert to dust. Send out your breath and life begins; you renew the face of the earth." Ezekiel (37:1–14) presents God's creative and life-giving breathing in a dramatic way, as the dry bones come clattering together, are covered with sinews and flesh and skin, and as breath enters them, the dead are brought back to life. It is such a vivid imaging of God's transforming power in bringing the house of Israel back to life.[78] The gift of the Spirit is a new creation. It gives a new identity to the disciples as children of God, born "from above", recalling the words of the Prologue (1:12–13) and Jesus' words to Nicodemus (3:3–10), and now able, as Jesus' brothers and sisters, to call God "Father" (20:17). The gift of the Spirit is the establishing of the New Covenant, creating the disciples as the New Israel.[79]

The Baptist indicated Jesus as "the one who would baptise with the Holy Spirit" (1:33), and Jesus, when addressing his followers during the final meal he shared with them, promised to send the Spirit (15:26). The giving of the Spirit is in the first place the disciples' consecration and empowerment for mission and ministry.[80] Secondly, it brings to a conclusion and climax the theme of water, life and Spirit, which has been running through the Gospel. This is the highpoint of Jesus' post-resurrection activity.[81] Most scholars discount Jesus' breathing forth his spirit on Calvary (19:30) as a giving of the Holy Spirit, and so this action in the room is the only giving of the Spirit in John. Others, however, are of the view that, as he dies, Jesus "hands over the Spirit", which is the first Spirit gift, making the post-resurrection gift in the room a second bestowal.[82] The Spirit is given as founding gift in 19:30, and as commissioning for witness and outreach in 20:22. Both aspects are part of the one Spirit gift in the "hour" of Jesus. The Spirit is not to dwell only with the new family brought into being at the cross. The disciples are to be for the world what Jesus has been, and so the community must reach beyond its own borders to continue Jesus' mission.[83]

The mission is then rendered more specific in terms of the forgiving and retaining of sins.[84] Just what this means and how this power is to be exercised has been divisive in Christianity over the years.[85] Brown believes that it may involve "an initial forgiveness by admission to baptism, and a continuing exercise of forgiveness within the bonds of Christian community life."[86] However, sin in the Fourth Gospel has primarily to do with being blind to God's revelation through Jesus' words and works, and refusing to believe in him.[87] Jesus is sent into the world by a loving God so that those who believe might be saved, might have eternal life. As the light of the world, Jesus inevitably creates a situation of judgement, for some accept him and others refuse to do so (3:16–21; 9:39). The disciples will continue to exercise in the world the critical presence of Jesus and his revelation, bringing into the darkness a light that is sometimes accepted, sometimes rejected, with consequences.[88] In his prayer at the Supper, Jesus acknowledges that the presence of his disciples in the world will cause some to believe and others to reject their message (17:14, 20). "The disciples both by deed and word cause people to judge themselves: some come to the light and receive forgiveness; some turn away and are hardened in their sins."[89] Like Jesus, the word and lifestyle-witness of the disciples as signs of God's presence and love in the world make it possible for people to accept the offer of entering into a relationship with God or to refuse it. This decision leads to the forgiving or retaining of sins.[90] The mission of the Paraclete is to "lay bare" the goodness and evil of the world (16:7–11), and it is through the gift of the Spirit that the disciples are empowered by the risen Jesus to be agents of forgiveness. This is part of the new creation.[91]

The Second Appearance

John's presentation of the resurrection of Jesus continues, as he personifies in Thomas the aspect of doubt that is a constituent part of the resurrection appearance narrative template. From a structural point of view, the appearance to the group (20:19–23) and then to Thomas (20:26–29) form a diptych, as words and actions mirror each other across the scenes. The refusal of Thomas to accept the witness of the disciples "We have seen the Lord" (20:24–25) is transitional and acts as a narrative hinge.[92] The text reads:

> But Thomas (who was called the Twin), one of the twelve, was not with them when Jesus came. So the other disciples told him, "We have seen the Lord." But he said to them, "Unless I see the mark of the nails in his hands, and put my finger in the mark of the nails and my hand in his side, I will not believe."

> A week later his disciples were again in the house, and Thomas was with them. Although the doors were shut, Jesus came and stood among them and said, "Peace be with you." Then he said to Thomas, "Put your finger here and see my hands. Reach out your hand and put it in my side. Do not doubt but believe." Thomas answered him, "My Lord and my God!" Jesus said to him, "Have you believed because you have seen me? Blessed are those who have not seen and yet have come to believe." (20:24–29)

The reader is now informed that Thomas, the twin, was not present with the other disciples when Jesus appeared to them. No reason is offered for his absence. He has not been part of the previous events: Magdalene's message, the appearance of Jesus and the Spirit gift. He has, however, played a role earlier in the narrative. When, following the delay after the death of Lazarus and the message from his sisters, Martha and Mary, Jesus finally decides to journey to Bethany, Thomas, aware of the mortal danger that this would entail for the Master, declares to the others: "Let us also go, that we may die with him." Though he does not fully understand what is happening, this is not simply wild bravado. It expresses his commitment to Jesus as best he knows how (11:16). Later, at the Supper, when Jesus speaks of going away and preparing a place for them, Thomas, clearly a practical man, says: "Lord, we do not know where you are going, so how can we know the way?" His question provokes that beautiful reply: "I am the way, and the truth and the life ... If you know me you will know my Father also. From now on you do know him and have seen him" (14:6–7). To see Jesus is to see God.[93] Jesus is going to the Father's house, and he is the way there for others; he enables his followers to know the Father and to share his life.[94]

Naturally, when Thomas rejoins the group, the others tell him of their remarkable and life-changing encounter.[95] It is an experience that must be shared. The verb is imperfect, which can indicate repetition (they kept telling him), or it can be conative (they attempted to tell him). They, of course, are filled with peace and joy, Spirit-filled and commissioned, and, echoing Magdalene's words, with enthusiasm they claim: "We have seen the Lord." The language is typical of the early Christian confessions.

Thomas, however, is still in the darkness of unfaith, and categorically refuses to believe; the verb comes at the end of the Greek sentence, and so is very strong.[96] Laying down clear conditions, he states that he will not believe unless he can see the holes made by the nails in Jesus' hands, put his finger right into the holes and place his hand into his side.[97] A link is established with Jesus' showing his hands and side to the disciples in his appearance. Thomas is demanding more than was offered to the other disciples, and indeed more than was necessary. The others saw and came to faith; he wishes to feel as well; he demands the most palpable evidence.[98] There is a parallel with Magdalene's search for physical experience and also her faith journey.[99] Thomas refuses to believe the witness of the other disciples.[100]

A week has gone by.[101] The disciples are still (or again) in the house in Jerusalem, and the doors are closed, but there is no mention of fear this time. Thomas is with them. Jesus again comes and stands among them and says: "Peace be with you." Jesus is aware of Thomas' demands, of course, and singles him out, quoting his words back to him: "Put your finger here; look, here are my hands.[102] Give me your hand; put it into my side. Do not be unbelieving any more but believe."[103] Jesus offers what Thomas requested but also commands him to reach beyond his conditioned faith. Perhaps Jesus' words were not meant to be taken literally but were ironic. We are not told that Thomas actually did as invited.[104] Jesus' final words suggest that sight was enough. In fact, had he accepted and probed the wounds, he could not have become a believer in the Johannine sense.[105]

Thomas accepts the challenge and makes his confession of faith: "My Lord and my God." He goes beyond the miraculous aspect of the appearance and sees what the Resurrection reveals about Jesus.[106] He concludes his faith journey; "the last word spoken by a disciple in the Gospel is an expression of full Christian faith."[107] The combination "Lord and God" is found in pagan religious literature; Domitian (81–96 CE), the emperor of the time, wished to be addressed in this way. But John's source is biblical. It combines the two terms commonly used in the LXX to translate Yahweh and Elohim (*kyrios* and *theos*). The LXX usually has "Lord, my God".[108] Psalms 35:23 says: "My God and my Lord."

This is the supreme Christological pronouncement and climax of the Fourth Gospel, proclaimed by one who was originally a professed doubter.[109] This Christological affirmation corresponds to the Christology developed in the whole Gospel narrative, recognising the implications of the Logos in the Prologue, the 'I am' sayings, and the claims that "the Father and I are one" (10:30). Thomas addresses Jesus in the same language in which Israel addressed Yahweh. The true identity of Jesus has been recognised. The use of "God" for Jesus is a confession of faith, not a dogmatic formulation or a metaphysical statement (see Rev 4:11).[110] And Jesus recognises that Thomas has, in fact, come to faith: "You have believed." Seeing and believing are twinned.[111]

The episode concludes with a beatitude: "You believe because you can see me. Blessed are those who have not seen and yet believe."[112] Some take the first part as a question, slightly ironic, challenging Thomas to examine the nature of his belief, even though he has made a confession of faith.[113] Most opt for a statement, the more difficult reading, because it gives a better sense and because of the solemnity of the pronouncement; Jesus is declaring the truth.[114] Some prefer "you have believed" (perfect tense), "because you saw me".[115]

The contrast in these words, which strengthens the rhetorical force, is between belief through sight and belief without sight. The Beloved Disciple came to faith through seeing the garments in the tomb; Magdalene, the other disciples and now Thomas came to the joyful belief in the resurrection of Jesus and all that this entailed through seeing him—a joy not to be taken away (16:22). The evangelist, however, is addressing the wider audience of later generations who have not seen Jesus, and whose faith has arisen from the word and testimony of those who did see him and is the fruit of the disciples' mission (17:20). Theirs is a different type of faith, not based on sight, but by no means inferior, no less genuine, and bestowing equal joy. "This is faith in the full Johannine sense of the term."[116] It corresponds to the new invisible presence of Jesus through the Spirit.[117] Collins notes two significant aspects of this beatitude. First, to be blessed is to anticipate going to the Father (as in 13:17); "the beatitude speaks of eternal beatitude." Secondly, it has a hortatory purpose; it urges those who have not seen to believe.[118]

The writer of 1 Peter says: "Although you have not seen him, you love him; and even though you do not see him now, you believe in him and rejoice with an indescribable and glorious joy" (1:8). But the Beloved Disciple, too, came to belief without seeing the risen Jesus; he saw the grave cloths, and this was enough. He makes it clear what it means to be a beloved disciple; he shows the way. Our faith matches his. But, unlike him, we have the book, a written witness, which we call the Gospel of John.[119] The blessing of Jesus empowers future disciples to share in his mission and enter a covenant relationship with God.[120] "Those upon whom the Revealer imparts a final blessing are none other than those who faithfully read the Fourth Gospel today."[121]

Reflections

There are several themes to ponder in these two room narratives. Immediately, the reader is again confronted with the fear of the disciples, the kind of fear that perhaps was responsible for their failure, a fear of arrest and punishment by the religious authorities. For the original hearers and readers of the Gospel, that kind of danger may not have been far away; some members of the community may even have been unfaithful under persecution. In our world today, some of our brothers and sisters are experiencing persecution for their allegiance to Jesus. As we support them by our prayers, we humbly acknowledge the weakness of our own faith commitment and are grateful not to have to undergo that kind of drastic test. In the story, however, fear is quickly dissipated by the presence of Jesus and is replaced by peace and joy, and we can imagine that joy as horror, disillusionment and despair are transformed. Life does have a meaning, there is future, because Jesus is alive. Joy is meant to be a characteristic of all the disciples of Jesus—not so much the joy of the champagne fizz variety or raucous roars of laughter, but the joy which emanates from that deep awareness of being loved by God, and of God's abiding presence with us, a joy which therefore permeates every aspect of our lives.[122]

And fear is linked with unbelief. Throughout the Fourth Gospel, the evangelist highlights the theme of faith. In fact, the story of Jesus is told so that we might come to faith or have our faith deepened (20:31). The pattern of the resurrection narratives matches that of other sequences in the ministry. Some characters believe, others are hesitant and move slowly, others refuse to believe. The evangelist is constantly challenging his readers about our faith. We can probably empathise readily with Thomas, who struggles with unbelief, who wants proofs. I'm sure most of us would welcome a tangible visit from the risen Jesus, even if that doesn't quite fit the evangelist's ideal of faith! Whilst we may feel uncomfortable with aspects of the teaching and life of our Church, the foundation of our faith remains the love of God for us as revealed in Jesus. Faith is above all a relationship into which we have been drawn, a love story in which we are involved. That we must cling to.

One of the main themes in John's presentation of Jesus is his sense of mission. Two key words that punctuate the whole Gospel narrative are 'being sent' (*apostellein)* and 'coming'; these terms occur more than forty times. One of the key texts involves Nicodemus, who, on his nocturnal quest, acknowledges that Jesus has "come from" God. In the 'dialogue become discourse' which develops, Jesus sums up his mission in unforgettable terms: "For God so loved the world that he gave his only Son, so that everyone who believes in him may not perish but may have eternal life. Indeed, God did not send the Son into the world to condemn the world, but in order that the world might be saved through him" (3:16–17). The being sent, or coming, is also a giving, and is the expression of the Father's love for the world. Its purpose is our salvation, or, equivalently, our new birth, our sharing in "eternal life", the very life of God.

Soon after in the narrative, when the disciples return to the well of Sychar, laden with food after their shopping expedition, and they press Jesus to eat, his response surprises them: "My food is to do the will of the one who sent me, and to complete his work" (4:34). This is such a powerful expression of the unwavering focus of his life. Still later, when speaking to the people in the Capernaum synagogue after the multiplication of the loaves and fish, Jesus states: "I have come from heaven not to do my own will, but to do the will of him who sent me" (6:38). On the final day of the feast of Tabernacles, Jesus claims: "If God were your Father, you would love me, for I came from God and now I am here. I did not come on my own, but he sent me" (8:42). And so it continues until the Calvary scene, when the "hour" has indeed come. After his cry of thirst, the soldiers kindly offer him some of their poor-quality wine. "When Jesus had received the wine, he said, 'It is finished.' Then he bowed his head and handed over the Spirit" (19:30 AT). The last words of Jesus are a cry of triumph: "mission accomplished!" He has fulfilled the scriptures; he has carried out to the last detail what he was sent to do. His final words echo his prayer to the Father at the Supper: "Father, I glorified you on earth by finishing the work that you gave me to do" (17:4). For the Fourth Evangelist, Jesus is totally referred to the Father, and totally taken up with mission. The two go together like the two sides of the same coin.

And the risen Jesus now involves his disciples in the sharing of his mission. As the Father has sent him, he now sends them, and he empowers them with the gift of the Spirit. We have received the Spirit-gift at our baptism, and that gift shapes our identity as disciples. Through the Spirit we are able to call God our Father, just as Jesus did. Through the Spirit we are drawn into the relationship of "abiding", an amazing mutuality and oneness, sharing the very life of God. And through the Spirit we become "sent ones". As with Jesus, relationship and mission go together in our lives. Reaching out to share our experience of the presence of the risen One in our lives is not an option, it is intrinsic to our personhood, a 'must do'.

The most amazing lesson of all is the revelation of love. The love of Jesus for "his own", love to the end and the fullest, seen especially in his giving his life for the sheep, is again manifest in his encountering them. The signs of his self-gift are present on his body. He comes to them in their immense fragility and failure and fear; he returns as promised, and does so with complete forgiveness, transforming their lives. That quality of love Jesus extends to us too. We are no less blessed than they. Sometimes our awareness of that love and of Jesus' abiding presence deep within us, and our abiding in him, can grow faint, and so the level of our aliveness becomes weak and fitful. But he still calls us his "friends"; he will always remain faithful. And at the end he will come again and take us to himself, so that we can be where he is, in the Father's house (14:1–3), and the aliveness which we share with him now will reach definitive fulfilment.

Notes

1   See, for example, Charles H. Dodd, *The Interpretation of the Fourth Gospel* (Cambridge: Cambridge University Press, 1963), 440, and Rudolf Bultmann, *Theology of the New Testament*. Translated by Kendrick Grobel. 2 vols. (London: SCM Press, 1955), 2, 56). The inclusion of narratives is a concession to established tradition.

2   Schneiders, *Jesus Risen*, 40–41. On p. 102, she notes that the distinction (theological, not chronological) is between what happened to Jesus on the cross (glorification) and the communication of the significance and effects of Jesus' glorification to the disciples (resurrection). In *Written That You May Believe* (New York: Crossroad, 1999), 190, she points out that the primary purpose of John 20 is not to tell the reader what happened to Jesus after his death, but to explore, through the paradigmatic and foundational experiences of the disciples, the effect on and meaning for believers of Jesus' glorification.

3   C. Kingsley Barrett, *The Gospel According to John* (London: SPCK, 1978), 459.

4   Francis J. Moloney, *The Gospel of John*. Sacra Pagina 3 (Collegeville, MN: Liturgical Press, 1998), 515–17.

5   Schneiders, *Jesus Risen*, 41. Moloney, *Resurrection*, 107, maintains that there are elements in the main Gospel story which remain unresolved. The resurrection narratives address the consequences of the "hour" for Jesus, and the consequences for believers. On p.152, he suggests that the story in John is more about what the risen Jesus does for the disciples than what God has done for Jesus.

6   Moloney, *John*, 517; Raymond E. Brown, *The Gospel according to John*. 2 vols. Anchor Bible (London: Chapmans, 1972), 2, 965; Mary L. Coloe, *Dwelling in the Household of God* (Collegeville, MN: Liturgical Press, 2007), 187, n.78; Schneiders, *Written*, 190; in *Jesus Risen*, 83–85, as well as this literary structure, she highlights a theological and spiritual structure, which answers the questions: "Where is the Lord?" and "How can he be encountered today?"

7 See Moloney, *John*, 516, for details; Dorothy A. Lee, *Flesh and Glory: Symbolism, Gender and Theology in the Gospel of John* (New York: Crossroad, 2002), 220–221, notes some of the literary problems that indicate the presence of editorial seams; John is modifying earlier traditions. See also Barnabas Lindars, *The Gospel of John* (London: Oliphants, 1972), 595, who suggests three traditions: the finding of the empty tomb by the women; a visit of Peter to the tomb; an appearance of Jesus to the assembled apostles.

8 Schneiders, 'The Resurrection (of the Body) in the Fourth Gospel: A Key to Johannine Spirituality', 169, notes how our only access to the meaning of what happened is the story itself. "The reader's interaction with the text gives rise to meaning that transforms the reader into the believer who has life in Jesus' name."

9 John 19:38–42. The theme of Jesus as King is prominent in the Johannine passion, especially in the Roman trial, and the polyglot notice fixed to the cross. Jesus reigns from the cross. The garden of burial now becomes the garden of life. For Lee, *Flesh and Glory*, 227, the garden is a symbol of fecundity and life. For Schneiders, *Jesus Risen*, 48, the setting evokes the creation narrative in Genesis (Gen 2:15–17; 3:8; 3:15), and the Canticle of Canticles (3:1–4), the hymn of the covenant between Yahweh and Israel. In *Written*, 195, she suggests that this is the garden of new creation and new covenant; the woman is symbolically the Johannine community.

10 Moloney, *John*, 521.

11 Lee, *Flesh and Glory*, 220–226. She does not realise that Jesus is "the resurrection and the life". Andrew T. Lincoln, *The Gospel according to Saint John* (New York: Crossroad, 2005), 488, draws attention to the frequency with which the tomb is mentioned; the focus changes to Jesus in v.16.

12 See 13:23–26; 19:25–27, where he plays a significant role in the story. In 18:15–16 the text refers to "the other disciple." Francis J. Moloney, *Love in the Gospel of John* (Grand Rapids, MI: Baker Academic, 2013), 172, notes that the phrase "whom Jesus loved" is here added for clarity to the original "the other disciple"; the two are the same person.

13 Some take Mary's use of the plural "we" as an indication of the presence of other women with her, as in the Synoptic tradition. John has omitted them because he prefers to have Jesus encounter individuals. Moloney, *John*, 518–519, however, maintains that Mary is associating the two male disciples with her lack of faith at this stage in the story. Awareness of an empty tomb does not automatically lead to resurrection faith. Something more is needed. For Schneiders, *Jesus Risen*, 46, the suggestion is that the problem is not merely personal but communal and carries ecclesiological freight. Craig R. Koester, *Symbolism in the Fourth Gospel* (Minneapolis: Fortress, 2003), 68, notes that many commentators see the plural (frequent in John) as an indication of representative significance. See also R. Alan Culpepper, *The Gospel and Letters of John* (Nashville: Abingdon Press, 1998), 239. Schneiders, *Written*, 191, recalls the importance in John of the word "where" (*pou*

and *hopou* in Greek, found 18 and 30 times). "Mary Magdalene voices the question of all disciples caught in the pre-dawn darkness of the scandal of the cross." The answer is given by the Beloved Disciple, and by Jesus' return to his own.

14   Moloney, *Resurrection,* 107, notes that the twofold use of the passive indicates that someone other than Jesus has entered the story. On p.152, he comments that Magdalene is correct in suggesting that someone has entered the realms of death and "taken away" Jesus from the tomb; this is not by stealth, but by resurrection. In *Love,* 163, he observes that "the action of God is present in the allusions to Jesus' resurrection in John 20: Jesus has been raised by God." In this John is in line with the other Gospels and the rest of the New Testament. The reader may recall mention of resurrection in 2:22; 12:16. Rekha M. Chennattu, *Johannine Discipleship as a Covenant Relationship* (Peabody, MA: Hendrickson, 2006), 142–143, links the *where (pou)* with the question of the first disciples in 1:38, and sees a theological meaning here (Jesus' communion with the Father) as well as a geographical significance. Schneiders, 'The Resurrection (of the Body) in the Fourth Gospel: A Key to Johannine Spirituality', 183, states that Magdalene voices the position of one who has not grasped the meaning of "the hour", Jesus' transition from the dispensation of the flesh to the dispensation of glory.

15   Koester, *Symbolism,* 68; *The Word of Life: A Theology of John's Gospel* (Grand Rapids, MI: Eerdmans, 2008), 124.

16   Here we touch a solid core of early Christian tradition in its simplest form. See Brown, *John,* 2, 998; in 2, 998–1014, he links John with traditions in the Synoptics about women followers going to the tomb, disciples (especially Peter) going to the tomb, and an appearance to the women. Luke 24:12: "But Peter got up and ran to the tomb; stooping and looking in, he saw the linen cloths by themselves; then he went home, amazed at what had happened." Schneiders, *Written,* 182, espouses the view that this verse is an interpolation or an assimilation of Luke to John. "Some of those who were with us went to the tomb, and found it just as the women had said; but they did not see him" (24:24). Peter may well have been among this group.

17   Lincoln, *John,* 490, observes that a secondary function of the introduction of two male disciples might be the supplying of two male witnesses, supplementing the dubious witness of a woman (Deut 19:15). On p. 489 he suggests a link with the relationship of Johannine Christians with the wider Church; the community is at one with the wider Church, but the stress is on the superior insight and unique contribution of the Johannine Christians and their Christology. Schneiders, *Written,* 183, observes that the two disciples are together physically at the beginning of the episode, and together spiritually in their ignorance of scripture at the end. Moloney, *John,* 519, says that they turn their backs on the situation in which they found themselves through their association with the unfaith of Magdalene, and move towards the place of the action of God (an empty tomb). He sees this as partial faith.

18   Lindars, *John*, 600--601; it thus builds up to the climax of the Beloved Disciple's belief; also, Brown, *John*, 2, 1007. Schneiders, *Written*, 184–85, suggests that in order to identify the face veil as a genuine sign, the evangelist has to present the Beloved Disciple's experience in two steps, using Peter's experience as a foil. Both see the cloths (the Beloved Disciple from outside, Peter from inside); Peter sees the face veil, and then the disciple, on entering, also does and believes. It is the face veil which is the cause of faith. The veil is a genuine Johannine *sign*. The journey or race to the tomb fits awkwardly into the narrative. The evangelist is modifying earlier traditions by inserting the passage about the two disciples into the Magdalene story. He wishes to locate the Beloved Disciple, the source of the Johannine tradition and a founder member of the community, in this important setting. Brown, *John*, 2, 1007: "the disciple who was bound closest to Jesus in love was the quickest to look for him and the first to believe in him."

19   Again, the passive is used; the signs of death have been removed (Moloney, *Resurrection*, 108). Lincoln, *John*, 490, notes the difference with Lazarus, who had to be freed from the head cloth and body wrappings. There is also an apologetic point: if the body had been stolen, the cloths would not have been taken off and neatly left behind. Brown, *John*, 2, 1007, acknowledges this view; also, Koester, *Word*, 124. Schneiders, *Written*, 182, comments that what is specific to John's account is the role of the Beloved Disciple in relation to Simon Peter and the presence of the burial cloths, especially the face veil in the tomb.

20   Schneiders, *Written*, 180–186; *Jesus Risen*, 47, links the face cloth with the veil of Moses in Exod 34:33–35; Moses lays aside the veil when ascending to meet God, Jesus likewise. But whereas Moses took up the veil again when returning to the people, Jesus has definitively laid aside the veil of the flesh as he ascends into the presence of God to receive the glory he had as Son before the world began (17:24). She considers the empty tomb and face cloth as a sign, revealing Jesus' glorification, his return to the Father. This is where he is. (also, in *Jesus Risen*, 183.) The sign is ambiguous (Peter failed to interpret it correctly). In *Jesus Risen*, 47, she suggests that what the Beloved Disciple believed was that on the cross, though he truly died, Jesus was exalted into the presence of God (see 13:1; 16:28; 17:1, 24). The face cloth of his flesh (i.e., his mortality in which his glory had been veiled during his pre-Easter career) is now definitively laid aside. "Jesus, the New Moses, has gone up the mountain to seal the New Covenant between God and the New Israel."

21   Schneiders, *Written*, 186, notes that if the veil is a *sign*, belief is the correct response; "it is a faith response to revelation encountered in sign."

22   Moloney, *Resurrection*, 110, notes that the beloved disciple comes to faith without seeing Jesus and without the scripture (i.e. the Gospel yet to be written). Lincoln, *John*, 491, sees this as the most likely interpretation; though he suggests that the scripture might be Psalms 16:10 (as in Acts 2:27). The disciple's insight is mentioned for the sake of the reader, and not passed on to those in the story. The reader does know the scripture (John's Gospel); see Chennattu, *Discipleship*, 146;

Culpepper, *John*, 240. Koester, *Word*, 125, observes that the faith of the Beloved Disciple does not include understanding or prompt him to say anything. Schneiders, *Written*, 192, believes the scripture concerns Jesus' resurrection from the dead, his return to his own. The first part of the answer is that Jesus is glorified in returning to the Father, the second is his return to his own in resurrection.

23   There is considerable scholarly debate about the quality of the Beloved Disciple's faith. Some, like Moloney, *Resurrection*, 110; *Love*, 172–173, understand it as full resurrection faith, reached without an appearance of the risen Jesus, a model for later disciples like us. For we, like him, do not see, but we can, unlike them, understand the scriptures. His faith is based on his interpretation of the face veil, folded and left on one side, recalling the veil of Moses and/or that of Lazarus. Schneiders, *Written*, 181, notes that the Beloved Disciple came to full paschal faith on the basis of what he saw in the tomb before any of Jesus' appearances. "The paschal believing of the Beloved Disciple is the faith response to revelation encountered as sign," (p.186). Having seen, he believes that Jesus has gone away and ascended to God (is glorified). Other scholars maintain that his failure to communicate his faith to Mary, and the fact that the two disciples return to the place where they were before, point to a faith which is only partial. The disciple is aware that a mysterious action of God is involved, but he does not yet fully understand its import. Ignace de la Potterie, *The Hour of Jesus* (Slough: St. Paul Publications, 1989), 202–203, interprets it as the beginning of faith, not complete faith; returning home is a return to the previous situation. Brown, *John*, 2, 1004–1007, deals with various views concerning the relationship in the narrative between Peter and the Beloved Disciple. He denies a deprecatory attitude to Peter; John wishes to emphasise the Beloved Disciple's primacy of love: "he was the quickest to look for him and the first to believe in him."

24   Moloney, *Resurrection*, 108–109; *Love*, 171, notes the depiction of the faith journey of four characters in the resurrection narratives (as with other individuals in the earlier part of the Gospel story): the Beloved Disciple, Peter, Thomas and Magdalene, three of them foundational for the community; they "bridge the gap between the story of Jesus and subsequent generations of Johannine disciples." Also, Koester, *Symbolism*, 68. Schneiders, *Jesus Risen*, 47, indicates the transition from the Jesus who is glorified and with God, to the Jesus who is also risen from the dead. In *Written*, 193–94, she makes the point that the appearance to Magdalene is not, as has been traditionally maintained, minor, private, personal and unofficial; for John, she is the recipient of the first Easter Christophany, the apostolic witness upon whom the paschal faith of the community was founded.

25   Schneiders, *Written*, 192–201. She sees these as structural: 11–15, 16, 17–18.

26   The verb (*klaiō*) is used four times. Jesus in 16:19–22 predicts a period of weeping and mourning that would give way to joy in seeing him (Lincoln, *John*, 492). See also Chennattu, *Discipleship*, 147; she notes on p.177 John's use of the promise-

94

fulfilment motif, which is essential to the covenant materials of the Old Testament. The promises of chapters 13–17 are fulfilled in chapters 20–21.

27   Lee, *Flesh and Glory*, 223.

28   De la Potterie, *Hour*, 210.

29   Lincoln, *John*, 492.

30   For Moloney, *Resurrection*, 110, her disposition at this stage is one of unfaith.

31   1:38. Jesus also asks this question in the garden (18:4). "Seeking" Jesus is an important concept in John (6:24–26; 13:33). Schneiders, *Resurrection*, 183, sees Jesus as the divine gardener inaugurating the new creation, the Shepherd, and the Spouse of the new covenant rewarding the search of the anguished lover.

32   An alternative view suggests that Mary, grieving and confused, is still in control. She wants information; she will solve the problem, set things right, and do it herself.

33   In the Synoptic tradition the angel(s) interpret the significance of the empty tomb and proclaim the basic kerygma; this is not the case in John. Chennattu, *Discipleship*, 148–149, sees links with Exod 37:5–7, and the image and role of the two guarding cherubim: they reveal the living presence of the covenant God in the empty tomb. Also, Schneiders, *Written*, 195, refers to Exod 25:22 and 38:7–8; *Jesus* Risen, 48. Lee, *Flesh and Glory*, 223, holds that their posture suggests symbolically the ark of the covenant. Moloney, *John*, 528, considers this "fanciful".

34   John 10:3–5, 14–15, 27; Isa 43:1. Lincoln, *John*, 493: her absorption with the realm of the dead is broken. Lee, *Flesh and Glory*, 223, notes the importance of the double naming (Mary, Rabbouni); names in the ancient world evoke identity, presence and relationship. Koester, *Symbols*, 69, indicates the pivotal role of the word and hearing. This is true for later Christians. Schneiders, *Written*, 196, believes this is one of the most moving verses in the New Testament. She maintains that she is already facing Jesus when he calls her name. She has already spoken to him and heard his voice without recognising him. It is his use of her name which brings about conversion. This turning is not physical, but spiritual.

35   Lee, *Flesh and Glory*, 224. Some catch in the narrative strong hints of Cant 3:1–4.

36   Schneiders, 'The Resurrection (of the Body) in the Fourth Gospel: A Key to Johannine Spirituality', 197, n. 55, comments that "Teacher" is the quintessential identity of the historical Jesus in John, as the primary relationship to him is that of "disciple". This address by Mary, with her attempt to touch him physically, suggests that she is short of full Easter faith.

37   Brown, *John*, 2, 992–993, lists the many attempts at interpreting "do not cling to me". Lee, *Flesh and Glory*, 225, holds that the Greek means "do not go on

touching me", an ongoing sense. The problem is not her touching him, but her holding on to him. Schneiders, *Jesus Risen*, 55, maintains that the verb (*haptō*) means touch, not hold on to (*krateō*). She further notes that Magdalene erroneously thinks that the past dispensation has been reinstated. Things will be as they had always been. In *Written*, 197, she writes that the verb means "do not continue to touch me"; but the Greek emphasises the "me" rather than the verb; she is being told not to try to encounter him as if he were the earthly Jesus resuscitated. Jesus is directing her away from himself to the community of his brothers and sisters.

38   Brown, *John*, 2, 1012; Magdalene mistakes his appearance for his permanent presence. John's concept of ascending is different from Luke's. John is interested not in the terminus of the appearances but the terminus of the "hour".

39   De La Potterie, *Hour*, 212–213. Moloney, *Resurrection*, 111; *Love*, 173, sees movement from conditioned faith to full faith, as she abandons attachment to physical reality and proclaims Jesus as the risen Lord. Schneiders, *Written*, 198, suggests that Jesus is redirecting Mary's desire for union with himself from his physical or earthly body (which in any case no longer exists because it is the glorified Lord who stands before her in an appearance that is temporary) to the new locus of his presence in the world, that is, the community of his brothers and sisters, his disciples. (The text literally is "not me continue to touch ... but go to my brothers and sisters.") Lee, *Flesh and Glory*, 225, says "His return to the Father is incomplete until he confirms in full the gift of the Spirit."

40   The language of ascension in the following verse is confusing. Moloney, *John*, 529, considers Jesus to be in the midst of a process not yet concluded. Lincoln, *John*, 493, refers to "a temporary stop in the one movement of ascent"; the emphasis is on Jesus' return to the Father; and the later appearances are of the already ascended Jesus. Brown, *John*, 2, 1015, believes that this is not a reference to a time sequence at all, as if Jesus is 'in between' resurrection and ascension. "It is a theological statement contrasting the passing nature of Jesus' presence in his post-resurrectional appearances and the permanent nature of his presence in the Spirit." He is fitting a theology of resurrection/ascension that by definition has no dimensions of time and space into a narrative that is essentially sequential. Schneiders, *Written*, 198–199, notes that the mystery of Jesus' glorification takes place when Jesus is lifted up. "The Jesus Mary encounters in the garden is clearly the glorified Jesus." She translates Jesus' words about ascension as a rhetorical question ("Am I as yet not ascended?"), expecting a negative answer: "No, you are indeed ascended, that is, glorified." and therefore will be encountered in the community, not in his earthly body. As far as Mary is concerned in the narrative, Jesus has not yet ascended to the Father. While Mary realises that he is risen, she has not yet realised that he is glorified. In *Jesus Risen*, 110, she states that Ascension in the Lukan sense is not a Johannine category. There is no time interval in which Jesus is risen but not ascended. The time interval is in the experience of the disciples. In 'The Resurrection (of the Body) in the Fourth Gospel: A Key to Johannine Spirituality', 183, she notes

the scholarly paraphrastic translation: "*For you* I am not ascended to the Father." In Mary's perception he has not yet ascended, for she has not yet integrated into her realisation that Jesus is risen the fact that he has also been glorified.

41   Schneiders, *Written*, 199.

42   Chennattu, *Discipleship*, 152, 154–155, stresses the covenant relationship aspect of the narrative; a new covenant family is created. Lee, too, *Flesh and Glory*, 225, notes the covenantal overtones. See also Brown, *John*, **2**, 1017.

43   The Greek term has inclusive meaning. The circle of disciples in John is not limited to males. See Schneiders, *Written*, 199.

44   See Moloney, *John*, 518–529. "Rabbouni" and "Lord" recall 13:13; "Lord" recurs in 20:25, 28. Schneiders, *Jesus Risen*, 56, notes that the words of her announcement indicate that she has made the necessary transition.

45   Schneiders, *Written*, 200, observes that in John bearing witness is based on what one has seen and heard (3:11; 19:35); this is a creedal formula (see 1 Cor 9:1). Her role is akin to the Lukan Peter (22:31–32): after her conversion to confirm the faith of her brothers and sisters. On the basis of this, Jesus later commissions them.

46   Schneiders, *Written*, 200.

47   Mary, woman of faith, key witness, is a foundational member of the Johannine community. For Lee, *Flesh and Glory*, 226, this is the structural climax of ch. 20. Schneiders, *Written*, 201, describes her as symbolically both the Johannine community encountering its glorified saviour, and the official witness to that community of what God has done for it in the glorification of Jesus.

48   Schneiders, *Written*, 194–195. On pp.200–201 she emphasises Magdalene's role as official apostolic witness, who confirms the faith of the others. In *Risen Jesus*, 56, n. 38, she adds that her mission did not end when that of the other apostles began; she is the apostle commissioned to announce the resurrection to the Church. Lee, *Flesh and Glory*, 225, links Magdalene with the mother of Jesus. Both are named "woman"; they belong to the same foundational event of the "hour". On p.226, she notes that the Christophany she receives is a "protophany", set apart from subsequent apparitions. On p.228 she concludes that flesh, even in its risen form, is still symbolic of divine glory. The risen Christ, in the flesh, remains the definitive symbol of God, the true Icon sustaining all life, mortal and eternal. For her (p.229), Magdalene symbolises the Christian community in its struggle to believe and in its transfiguring reception of Easter faith. She becomes for the community of faith a symbol pointing to the living presence of Jesus, even in absence.

49   See John V. Taylor, *A Matter of Life and Death* (London: SCM Press, 1986), 62.

50   Henri Nouwen, *With Open Hands* (Notre Dame, IND: Ave Maria Press, 1972), 9–22, uses the symbolism of clenched fists and open hands with regard to prayer, but it can have a much wider application.

51   Schneiders, *Jesus Risen,* 48, notes a transition from the question "Where is the Lord?" to "How can the risen Lord be experienced?"

52   Schneiders, 'The Resurrection (of the Body) in the Fourth Gospel: A Key to Johannine Spirituality', 184, observes that the depth of this scene "derives largely from the fact that it is suffused with the Last Discourse(s) material, which itself is suffused with the themes and even the language of the New Covenant from Isaiah 51–56 and 65–66, Jeremiah 31, Ezekiel 36–37." She divides the scene into two parts: the Christophany and the giving of the Spirit.

53   Brown, *John,* 2, 1019, suggests that "that day" may evoke the Old Testament concept of the day of the Lord (Isa 52:6); perhaps John saw this Sunday as the eschatological day. The parallel with v.26 suggests that his presentation may have been influenced by the Christian custom of celebrating Eucharist on "the first day of the week" (Acts 20:7; 1 Cor 16:2). On 2, 1028–29, he notes the similarities with Luke 24:36–49, and believes that the two are probably independent developments of the original Jerusalem narrative. Schneiders, *Jesus Risen,* 106, draws attention to the three-part time indication: it evokes the historical day (Easter day), the eschatological ("that day"), and the liturgical (the first day of the week, the time of Christian Eucharist). The "day" of the present age, which ended with Christ's glorification on the cross, draws to a close as "that day", the eschatological day of the new dispensation inaugurated by Jesus' resurrection, dawns. The disciples are drawn into the mystery of Jesus' promised presence with them (14:20). This is the mystery experienced anew in Eucharist on Sundays down through the centuries.

54   Chennattu, *Covenant,* 158, n. 59, refers to 9:22, and suggests the possibility that this may reflect fear of persecution in the Johannine community at the time of composition of the Gospel; see R. Alan Culpepper, *The Gospel and Letters of John* (Nashville: Abingdon Press, 1998), 242; Lincoln, *John,* 497, who notes that the phrase is associated with an unwillingness to make a public confession about Jesus (7·13; 19:38; 9:22). Brown, *John,* 2, 1028, observes that Magdalene's faith has had no effect on the group, nor is there a trace of the Beloved Disciple's faith.

55   As in Matthew, Luke and 1 Cor 15:5. Brown, *John,* 2, 1034–35, holds that the pre-Gospel narrative referred to the eleven, but v.22, the evangelist's addition to the original narrative, suggests a widening of the horizon to include also those whom the Twelve represent. Chennattu, *Covenant,* 155, notes that some scholars believe that "disciples" refers to the inner circle; but there is no evidence in the Gospel that this is so. Barrett, *John,* 472–73, suggests that if it is the inner group, they are representative of the whole Church of the future. Moloney, *John,* 534, believes that disciples as such are intended here; the following scene is addressed to all disciples of Jesus. Schneiders, *Jesus Risen,* 90, 107, believes the term "disciples" refers to all Jesus' followers, the community, whomsoever it includes. On p.122, she notes that for John, "disciple" is a category which includes both women and men, is more extensive than the "Twelve," and is not equivalent to "apostles". Apostles are not mentioned in this Gospel; there is no calling of the Twelve or list of them, though John is aware

of the group (6:67–71; 20:24). On p. 178, she sees the Great Commission as given to the whole Church; "disciples" is an inclusive term, not restricted to the Twelve or the apostles. In 'The Resurrection (of the Body) in the Fourth Gospel: A Key to Johannine Spirituality', 186, she writes: "Believers, the Church as community and not as hierarchical institution, is the foundational symbolic expression of the risen Jesus. The Church is his body."

56   This may be seen as the fulfilment of the promise of 14:18, 28. Schneiders, *Jesus Risen*, 89, 108, 124–27, links the verb with 2:19–21: "Jesus was speaking of the temple of his body," and translates the text as "arose among" rather than "came and stood" (for details see p. 78, n.38). Jesus, now bodily risen, is the New Temple raised up in the midst of the community that will constitute the New Israel (see Ezek 37:26–28; 34:25; Isa 54:10) and will inaugurate the New Covenant. (He does not come through the door or walls!)

57   Brendan Byrne, *Life Abounding: A Reading of John's Gospel* (Strathfield, NSW: St Paul's, 2014), 334, believes that we are probably to understand that Jesus' ascension to the Father occurs between the appearance to Magdalene and this appearance to the disciples. The glorification of Jesus is now complete. See also Chennattu, *Covenant*, 161. This is the view also of De la Potterie, *Hour*, 216. He notes that the progressive revelation is not a detailed account of the exact sequence of events that constitute the Easter mystery (in both historical and transcendent unfolding); it is a catechetical and theological presentation, enabling us to understand little by little the multiple dimensions of the mystery.

58   De la Potterie, *Hour*, 216.

59   In the New Testament letters the normal greeting is "grace and peace to you". Chennattu, *Covenant*, 158–59, sees peace and covenant relationship as intimately related. "Jesus' blessing of peace prepares the disciples to become covenant partners with God." Similarly, Schneiders, *Jesus Risen*, 108; the New Covenant of peace is then linked with the signs of his glorification in his hands and side.

60   Brown, *John*, **2**, 1035; in *Risen Christ*, 74, he notes that in biblical Hebrew the *shalom* greeting tends to be confined to solemn, often revelatory moments.

61   According to Chennattu, *Covenant*, 158, many of the promises made by Jesus in chapters 13–17 are fulfilled in the narrative (14:18, 19; 15:11; 16:20–24). Similarly, Culpepper, *Gospel and Letters*, 242–43. Lincoln, *John*, 497, notes that the reception of this gift of peace provides a sense of ultimate security that no locked doors could assure.

62   Brown, *John*, **2**, 1021; Byrne, *Life Abounding*, 335; Culpepper, *Gospel and Letters*, 242; Moloney, *John*, 534.

63   Schneiders, *Jesus Risen*, 176. This peace takes away the "sin of the world". It enables the disciples to accept the utterly free and unconditional love of God, which they could never deserve or earn. "The risen Jesus, returned to his own in the full

integrity of his glorified humanity, is forgiveness incarnate, the very embodiment of reconciliation that is radical and permanent, of union with God, which is eternal life."

64   Barrett, *John*, 472, notes that Jesus was sufficiently corporeal to show his wounds and sufficiently immaterial to pass through closed doors. Jesus' feet are not mentioned. Schneiders, *Jesus Risen*, 49, 108, observes that the verb (*deiknymi)* denotes the revelatory rather than apologetic character of Jesus' action; he is marked with the signs of his paschal mystery; his bodyself is both continuous and discontinuous with the One they had known. "It is a revelatory identification of himself as the one who was glorified on the cross and whose Glorification is the source of the peace he has just imparted and the Spirit he is about to bestow." The significance of the open side touches the symbolism of temple, water and Spirit in the Fourth Gospel.

65   Moloney, *John*, 534. Schneiders, *Jesus Risen*, 106, calls the episode "The Revelatory Christophany".

66   Brown, *Risen Christ*, 74, suggests that the absence of doubt is intelligible because Magdalene has already told them that she has seen the Lord.

67   Schneiders, *Jesus Risen*, 49, n.30, notes that 14:28 uses the present tense "I go away and I come to you". This going away is necessary because as flesh, Jesus would be unable to establish the kind of mutual interiority with his disciples that he can in the Spirit who will be with them and in them (14:16–17). In 'The Resurrection (of the Body) in the Fourth Gospel: A Key to Johannine Spirituality', 184, she writes that Jesus "is alive with a new life that is bodily but no longer subject to death or to the laws of historical space, time and causality. He is the same person, Jesus, but in a new mode of being and presence."

68   "As you have sent me into the world, so I have sent them into the world." The two verbs for sending in 20:21 are different (*apostellein* and *pempein)*; Barrett, *John*, 473, states that they are used synonymously throughout the Gospel, but Brown, *Risen Christ*, 75, believes that this is not simply a typical stylistic variant; John does not use the noun "apostle" of the Twelve in a technical sense. In 13:16 it simply means someone who has been sent. Schneiders, *Jesus Risen*, 111–12, believes that there is a significant distinction between them. *Apostellein* emphasises the relation of the sent to those to whom one is sent, *pempein* the relation of the sent to the sender. The former is used of Jesus only twice (here and 5:36), the latter more than twenty times.

69   Lincoln, *John*, 498. Schneiders, *Jesus Risen*, 111, says that this second gift refers to the peace that will undergird their mission.

70   See 4:34; 5:36; 9:4; 17:4. Brown, *John*, 2, 1036; he states that the Father's sending of the Son is both model and ground for the Son's sending of the disciples. Schneiders, *Jesus Risen*, 111, considers it "foundation and pattern".

71   Moloney, *John*, 531.

100

72   Brown, *John,* **2**, 1036.

73   Brown, *Risen Christ,* 75, n. 90.

74   Chennattu, *Covenant,* 161. The adverb *kathōs* is used to express the intimate knowledge (10:14–15), love (15:9; 17:23), and communion (17:22) between Jesus and his disciples. Lincoln, *John,* 498, comments that "just as Jesus' mission entailed loving service to the point of giving his life, so the manner of his mission will be the pattern of his witnessing representatives". This point is reinforced by the display of his wounded hands and side.

75   Schneiders, *Jesus Risen,* 113, observes that "Having said this" shows the dependence of the commission on its foundation in Jesus' own mission from the Father.

76   Schneiders, *Jesus Risen,* 137-38, notes how the Baptist proclaims Jesus as the Lamb of God who takes away the sin of the world (1:29), and refers to the Spirit descending on Jesus and remaining on him, empowering him to fulfil this mission. Jesus now empowers his disciples through the gift of the Spirit for their mission.

77   The Greek word applies to Spirit, wind and breath. Culpepper, *Gospel and Letters,* 243, see Jesus' act of empowering for mission as almost a re-enactment of the creation scene in Genesis 2:7; similarly Barrett, *John,* 474; Lincoln, *John,* 499; and De la Potterie, *Hour,* 217, "at this moment a new and eschatological creation is taking place by the gift of the Spirit: the dawn of Easter faith in the hearts of the disciples is for them a new creation."

78   The verb (*emphysan*) is used only here in the New Testament, and twice in the Old (Gen 2:7; Ezek 37: 9–10). See also Wis 15:11; 1 Kings 19:11; Ezek 36:22–32; Isa 44:3; Hos 14:4.

79   Schneiders, *Jesus Risen,* 50. On p.113, she writes: "Jesus, in an act of New Creation, breathes the promised Spirit of the New Covenant into the community of his disciples, making them the New Israel, in whose midst he is present as the New Temple." The Spirit unites them to Jesus and empowers them for a new life in which they will continue Jesus' mission.

80   De la Potterie, *Hour,* 218–219, argues that the gift of the Spirit is bestowed first in order to arouse Easter faith; this is a precondition for effective mission.

81   Brown, *John,* **2**, 1037.

82   Moloney, *Resurrection,* 112. Chennattu, *Covenant,* 162, holds that "the bestowal of the Holy Spirit signals a new beginning of the covenant community, now sharing the life of God." Covenant language was used in 20:17.

83   Moloney, *John, 532;* in *Resurrection,* 112, he rightly points out that the Spirit gift, promised across the Gospel, and especially in the Paraclete sayings, cannot be limited to 20:22, which is closely tied to the authority of the disciples to

forgive and retain sin. It is not possible to harmonise John and Luke; each describes the same event from his own theological perspective. See Barrett, *John*, 475, who writes that "it is probable that to the first Christians the resurrection of Jesus and his appearances to them, his exaltation (however that was understood), and the gift of the Spirit, appeared as one experience, which only later came to be described in separate elements and incidents." Brown, *John*, 2, 1038–39, discusses the Johannine and Lukan presentations, concluding that the different descriptions reflect the diverse theological interests of the respective authors. Functionally, each is describing the same event; the one gift of the Spirit to his followers by the risen and ascended Lord. Lincoln, *John*, 500, notes that Luke spreads out the events chronologically and distinguishes between the episodes of resurrection, ascension and giving of the Spirit, John brings them all together on one day. For Schneiders, *Jesus Risen*, 113, this is the gift of the fullness of the Spirit who is the Paraclete promised by Jesus in the Last Discourses.

84   Brown, *John*, 2, 1023, observes that "if" can also be "when", and for "forgive" the aorist subjunctive is used, indicating an act that in a moment brings forgiveness; for "retain" the present is used, implying that the state of retaining continues. The passive indicates God's action. Chennattu, *Covenant*, 163–64, links forgiveness with the tradition of covenant renewal (Jer 31:34b; Ezek 26:25; Josh 24:14–15) and notes a link with Matthew's binding and loosing (18:18); see also Dodd, *Tradition*, 347–49; Lincoln, *John*, 500. Chennattu maintains that "the mission to forgive and retain sins must be interpreted in the light of Jesus' work to which all the disciples are called." Schneiders, *Jesus Risen*, 91–92, 115, 146–47, notes that the usual translation of the first part of the saying cannot be disputed. However, she maintains that the verb *kratein* in the second part never means to retain in classical or Koine Greek; and there is no direct object or indirect object in the Greek text. She translates: "Anyone whom you hold fast is held fast." It refers to people, not sins; it is not a parallel with Matt 18:18, who uses different verbs here and in 16:19; literary and theological contacts between the two are non-existent. (Besides, the Matthean texts refer to human interpretation of laws by religious authorities, not to the forgiveness of sins.) Those "forgiven" (in baptism) are "held fast" in the communion of the Church, for the mission of Jesus is frequently described in terms of preserving his disciples in union (6:37, 39; 10:28–29; 17:12; 18:9). "Sins" are expressions of the fundamental "sin". The charge therefore expresses the mission of the disciples in terms of continuing the mission of Jesus; similarly, in 'The Resurrection (of the Body) in the Fourth Gospel: A Key to Johannine Spirituality', 186–187; the disciples are to carry on the mission of receiving those whom the Father gives them and holding them fast in the community. The role of the community is not to exercise judgement, for Jesus was not sent for this (12:47). "The community in all its members is Jesus at work in the world and his work is to take away sins by giving life in all its fullness." Schneiders, *Jesus Risen*, 120, says "this text is not about the sacrament of penance." On p.92, n. 67, she notes that the only passage where the verbs *aphiēmi* and *krateō* occur together in reference to an object is Song 3:4: "I held him and would not let him go."

85   For a thoughtful study of the issues involved see Brown, *John*, 2, 1041–45; see also Schneiders, *Jesus Risen*, 114, 179–80, and n. 52.

86   Brown, *John*, 2, 1044. An established Church community would require forgiveness both at the time of a person's admission and afterwards. The gift of the Spirit is boundless (3:34). Barrett, *John*, 475, believes that there is probably a reference to baptism (as in Matt 28:19 and Mark 16:16), where the charge to baptise carries with it the offer of forgiveness; "the Church, by conferring or not conferring baptism, opens or closes the door of the redeemed community", but it is not restricted to baptism. Lincoln, *John*, 500, maintains that while post-baptismal sins cannot be excluded, the primary emphasis here seems to be the disciples' witness to the world. Schneiders, *Jesus Risen*, 117, suggests that later disciples who have been cleansed from "sin" by believing in Jesus, would be purified of their "sins", probably originally a reference to baptism, but perhaps also to sins committed after baptism. On p.181, she notes that with reference to forgiveness, the first verb (aorist) indicates a punctual act, the second (passive perfect) the resultant ongoing condition. In the second part of the text, John uses an active present subjunctive, which indicates an ongoing present behaviour, followed again by perfect passive (ongoing condition). Hence the idea is "those whom you are holding, (embracing or including in the ongoing life of the community) are indeed held fast in the communion of reconciliation."

87   For Schneiders, *Jesus Risen*, 139, the "sin of the world" is refusing to believe that God is love, not accepting the Gift of God that is Jesus.

88   Moloney, *Resurrection*, 131, n.35; *John*, 536; Brown, *Risen Christ*, 77.

89   Brown, *John*, 2, 1043.

90   Brown, *Risen Christ*, 77, writes: "To represent Christ to a degree that forces people to make a decision in their lives is a tremendous empowerment." Byrne, *Life Abounding*, 336, puts it this way: "As bearers of the Spirit the disciples are missioned to offer the world the reconciliation and eternal life won by the Son, whom the Father sent into the world not to condemn but so that the word might be saved through him (3:17). People who respond in faith, exposing their lives to the divine light and truth, find forgiveness of their sins and rebirth as members of the family of God. Those who refuse to believe and come to the light, bring down judgement upon themselves (3:18–19; 9:39–41; 5:24–29). In this sense, their sins are retained." Along similar lines, De la Potterie, *Hour*, 219, refers to "discrimination" (9:39); "their ministry of pardon will be the actualisation of Christ's sacrifice and of his salvation, for, as the Good Shepherd, Jesus 'gives his life for the sheep' (10:15)." Brown, *John*, 2, 1044, refers to the "power to isolate, repel and negate evil and sin, a power given to Jesus by the Father and given in turn by Jesus through the Spirit to those whom he commissions."

91   Schneiders, *Jesus Risen*, xviii, suggests that the commission of the disciples is to continue the mission of Jesus to take away the sin that prevents people from participating in the New Covenant which Jesus has established. In 'The Resurrection (of the Body) in the Fourth Gospel: A Key to Johannine Spirituality', 186, she notes

that the text never mentions Jesus leaving his disciples, which suggests the new mode of his presence with his disciples.

92   Coloe, *Household of God*, 170–171. The parallelism between the two appearance stories is noted also by De la Potterie, *Hour*, 224. Raymond F. Collins, 'Blessed are those who have not seen: John 20:29', in *Transcending Boundaries*, eds R. M. Chennattu and M. L. Coloe (Rome: LAS, 2005), 184, also notes that the two scenes describing the appearance of the risen Jesus form a diptych whose hinge is the description of the meeting of Thomas with the other disciples. The second appearance scene is basically a doublet of the first.

93   Koester, *Word of Life*, 127.

94   Coloe, *Household of God*, 170, suggests that in John 11 and 14 Thomas comes across as "particularly obtuse." Barrett, *John*, 476, thinks the earlier references suggest a "loyal but obtuse, rather than a doubtful and hesitating, character."

95   Thomas is introduced as "one of the Twelve". The only individuals identified in this way in the whole Gospel are Thomas and Judas (6:71). The Synoptists mention the doubt of the disciples as a group (Matt 28:17; Lk 24:11, 41; Mk 16:14). Collins, 'Blessed are those who have not seen', 187, sees Thomas as a foil, made to bear the doubt of the disciples, a representative figure.

96   The doubt, non-recognition element of the Appearance Narrative pattern, omitted in the previous episode, now receives a full and dramatic development and is personified in Thomas. This is a creation of the evangelist, who has transferred the traditional doubt element to create a separate narrative with some new elements. See Brown, *John*, 2, 1031. De la Potterie, *Hour*, 224, notes that the witness of the other disciples ought to have been enough for Thomas; he should have believed without seeing.

97   The verb (*ballein*) indicates more than simply "place"; "It conveys the idea of an energetic thrust." (Moloney, *John*, 539; Brown, *John*, 2, 1025). Brown, *John*, 2, 1033, observes that there is a more explicit concentration in the Thomas story on the nature of Jesus' body than in the appearance story.

98   In 4:48, Jesus rejects miracles demanded as an absolute condition for faith (Brown, *John*, 2, 1045; *Risen Christ*, 78).

99   Moloney, *Resurrection*, 113. Byrne, *Life Abounding*, 337, writes that like Mary in her attempt to cling to the body of Jesus, Thomas requires the crucified one to be present in full physical reality before he believes. Schneiders, *Jesus Risen*, 51, notes that Thomas wishes to return to the pre-Easter dispensation, relating to Jesus in the flesh. He is not a doubter, as popularly acclaimed, but an unbeliever.

100   Lincoln, *John*, 503.

101   Brown, *Risen Christ*, 78, suggests that this may indicate a reverence for Sundays in the Johannine community, when Eucharist would probably be celebrated.

Rev 1:10 refers to "the Lord's day". See also Culpepper, *The Gospel and Letters of John*, 242; Barrett, *John*, 476, suggests the possibility of a special intention in John's account of the Lord's special presence on the first day of the week, the day of the Church's regular assembly. On p. 477, he suggests that the whole passage from v.19 may be liturgical in origin. Coloe, *Household*, 171–187, explores in detail the relationship of the scene to the eucharistic gatherings of the Johannine community; similarly, Schneiders, *Jesus Risen*, 51. In this context, Brown, *John*, 2, 1047, suggests that Thomas speaks the doxology on behalf of the Christian community.

102   The verb is "see", which is part of a revelation formula in John. Schneiders, *Jesus Risen*, 52, writes: "The wounds of Jesus are not a proof of physical reality but the source of a true understanding of the meaning of Jesus' revelatory death."

103   De la Potterie, *Hour*, translates as "Become a man of faith"; Barrett, *John*, 476, suggests "Show that you do believe." Lincoln, *John*, 502, notes that there is no verb of doubting here; Jesus invites Thomas to change from being unbelieving to believing.

104   Brown, *John*, 2, 1046, states that "Thomas comes to belief without probing Jesus' wounds." Lincoln, *John*, 503, notes that there is no indication that Thomas takes up Jesus' invitation; similarly, Dunn, *Jesus Remembered*, 851.

105   Schneiders, *Jesus Risen*, 52, notes that John's Jesus is not like Luke's, proving that he is not a ghost but is inviting Thomas to grasp in faith what his saving death means and appropriate in faith the fruits of that death: the Spirit poured forth from his open side.

106   Brown, *John*, 2, 1047.

107   Brown, *John*, 2, 1032. Lincoln, *John*, 503, notes that this is the first time that a character in the story calls Jesus 'God', though readers have known this from the Prologue (1:1). Koester, *Word of Life*, 127, observes that by calling Jesus "my Lord", Thomas makes his own what he heard from the disciples, who said they had seen "the Lord." By calling Jesus "my God", he makes his own what he heard at the Last Supper, that seeing Jesus means seeing God.

108   See Gen 24:3, 12; Exod 3:15; 5:1; Lev 18:4; Deut 26:14. For Chennattu, *Covenant*, 166, these are expressions linked with the covenant relationship between God and Israel; Brown *John*, 2, 1048 also accepts the covenant aspect of this confession. Thomas' words are "the voice of the people ratifying the covenant which the Father has made in Jesus." Dunn, *Jesus Remembered*, 851, n. 110, comments that this is the climax not only of John's high Christology but of the second Christian generation's growing perception of who Jesus really was.

109   Byrne, *Life Abounding*, 337, calls this one of the Gospel's delightful paradoxes.

110   Brown, *John*, 2, 1047. Chennattu, *Covenant*, 166, writes that Thomas' confession of faith "epitomises the response of the new covenant community

recreated and empowered by the bestowal of the Holy Spirit that in Jesus they have experienced the fullness of God's revelation as their covenant God."

111   The two terms are repeated three times: vv. 25, 26a, 26b; the progression is no sight, no faith; sight, faith; no sight, faith. (Collins, 'Blessed are those who have not seen', 185).

112   Collins, 'Blessed are those who have not seen', 189, comments that in narrow focus the beatitude serves as the conclusion to the scene of the risen Jesus appearing to the disciples, Thomas being present (John 20:26–29). In broader focus, Jesus' logion is the conclusion to the entire Johannine narrative. This is the only pure beatitude in the Gospel, containing only five words in Greek; 13:17 he calls a borderline beatitude. On p.188, he notes that the commission in Matthew and the beatitude in John extend the narrative time of the evangelist's story beyond the story itself. He discusses the nature of a beatitude on pp.174–77, concluding that the evangelist composed this beatitude *ad hoc*.

113   See Chennattu, *Covenant*, 166. Lincoln, *John*, 501; NRSV and NAB.

114   Barrett, *John*, 477. Culpepper, *Gospel and Letters*, 244, considers this a higher level of faith.

115   Lincoln, *John*, 503, takes Jesus' words to mean "Have you believed their testimony because you have seen me? Blessed are those who have not seen but have believed their testimony", stressing the authority and reliability of the disciples' witness.

116   Collins, 'Blessed are those who have not seen', 188.

117   Brown, *John*, 2, 1048.

118   Collins, 'Blessed are those who have not seen", 188–89.

119   Moloney, *Resurrection*, 115–116; De la Potterie, *Hour*, 230, adds that the evangelist regards his work as a witness. Lincoln, *John*, 504, concludes: "Authentic faith is based on testimony, and the Gospel narrative itself, with its witness to Jesus' signs, including his resurrection, makes such faith available to later readers."

120   Chennattu, *Covenant*, 168. Brown, *John*, 2, 1051, notes that in the Jerusalem tradition found in Luke (24:51), Acts (1:9) and the Markan Appendix (16:19), Jesus departs; in John he remains present through the Paraclete (16:19).

121   Collins, 'Blessed are those who have not seen', 189. Schneiders, *Jesus Risen*, 105, comments that in John, unlike Luke's Emmaus story, there is no reference to Jesus vanishing. Jesus has definitively returned to "his own" and will never leave them. He has taken up his abode with them. In 'The Resurrection (of the Body) in the Fourth Gospel: A Key to Johannine Spirituality', 188, she says that "later disciples are to discern the new bodily presence of Jesus in the ecclesial community, Eucharist and Gospel. In all these cases Jesus, as the locus and revelation of God's

glory, is perceptible only to the eyes and ears of faith responding to the symbolic modes of his presence."

122   Our current Holy Father has reminded us vigorously of the pervasive joy of the Gospel in his Apostolic Exhortation *Evangelii Gaudium,* published in 2013.

Chapter Five
The Resurrection in John 21

After reflecting on the magnificent way in which the evangelist rounds off his story of Jesus, it comes as a surprise to turn the page and find a puzzling and fascinating reprise. We have read how Jesus, after encountering Magdalene in the garden, has appeared to the disciples in a Jerusalem room, breathed on them the Holy Spirit, and sent them on mission as he had himself been sent by the Father. The subsequent encounter between Jesus and Thomas concludes with a beatitude for those who believe without seeing, and there is a clear finality to the ending, summing up the purpose for which the Gospel has been written: "that you may believe that Jesus is the Messiah, the Son of God, and that through believing you may have life in his name."

Now, however, a group of the disciples are back in Galilee and are engaged in fishing, though there has not been any hint so far that this was their original occupation. Excited rejoicing or a vibrant sense of mission have dissipated. Jesus appears on the shore of the lake but, as if nothing has happened in Jerusalem, he is not initially recognised. The symbolism, too, is different. Fishing and hauling in the nets are central factors, picking up the traditional mission element of resurrection narratives. This is followed by the sharing of a meal. While there is a Christological element still, there is now a focus on Simon Peter and the Beloved Disciple, suggesting that the thrust in this chapter has to do with issues and responsibilities in the post-Easter community.[1]

Much Johannine scholarship in recent decades has been devoted to discussing the relationship between what many have come to call the 'Epilogue' and the previous twenty chapters of the Gospel, with their elements of continuity and discontinuity.[2] All agree that the Fourth Gospel was never circulated without this final chapter, but it is usually considered to be an addition to the original

Gospel, probably written by an author other than the one responsible for the main body of the Gospel, but a member of the same Johannine circle, the same thought world, who incorporates old and valuable tradition.³ As the Johannine community developed, its members were troubled by issues concerning the nature and mission of the community and questions of leadership and authority. John 21 is a response to this, and though written separately, it is integral to the whole work, forming a literary unit.⁴ Without it the Gospel would be much impoverished.⁵ It preserves the tradition of an appearance in Galilee, records the restoration of Peter, and clarifies the roles of Peter and the Beloved Disciple, before concluding with a strong statement concerning the value and truth of the written text.⁶

The text reads as follows:

> After these things Jesus showed himself again to the disciples by the Sea of Tiberias; and he showed himself in this way. Gathered there together were Simon Peter, Thomas called the Twin, Nathanael of Cana in Galilee, the sons of Zebedee, and two others of his disciples. Simon Peter said to them, "I am going fishing." They said to him, "We will go with you." They went out and got into the boat, but that night they caught nothing.

> Just after daybreak, Jesus stood on the beach; but the disciples did not know that it was Jesus. Jesus said to them, "Children, you have no fish, have you?" They answered him, "No." He said to them, "Cast the net to the right side of the boat, and you will find some." So they cast it, and now they were not able to haul it in because there were so many fish. That disciple whom Jesus loved said to Peter, "It is the Lord!" When Simon Peter heard that it was the Lord, he put on some clothes, for he was naked, and jumped into the lake. But the other disciples came in the boat, dragging the net full of fish, for they were not far from the land, only about a hundred yards off.

> When they had gone ashore, they saw a charcoal fire there, with fish on it, and bread. Jesus said to them, "Bring some of the fish that you have just caught." So Simon Peter went aboard and hauled the net ashore, full of large fish, a hundred and fifty-three of them; and though there were so many, the net was not torn. Jesus said to them, "Come and have breakfast." Now none of the disciples dared to ask him, "Who are you?" because they knew it was the Lord. Jesus came and took the bread and gave it to them, and did the same with the fish. This was now the third time that Jesus appeared to the disciples after he was raised from the dead.

> When they had finished breakfast, Jesus said to Simon Peter, "Simon son of John, do you love me more than these?" He said to him, "Yes, Lord; you know that I love you." Jesus said to him, "Feed my lambs." A second time he said to

him, "Simon son of John, do you love me?" He said to him, "Yes, Lord; you know that I love you." Jesus said to him, "Tend my sheep." He said to him the third time, "Simon son of John, do you love me?" Peter felt hurt because he said to him the third time, 'Do you love me?' And he said to him, "Lord, you know everything; you know that I love you." Jesus said to him, "Feed my sheep. Very truly, I tell you, when you were younger, you used to fasten your own belt and to go wherever you wished. But when you grow old, you will stretch out your hands, and someone else will fasten a belt around you and take you where you do not wish to go." (He said this to indicate the kind of death by which he would glorify God.) After this he said to him, "Follow me."

Peter turned and saw the disciple whom Jesus loved following them; he was the one who had reclined next to Jesus at the supper and had said, "Lord, who is it that is going to betray you?" When Peter saw him, he said to Jesus, "Lord, what about him?" Jesus said to him, "If it is my will that he remain until I come, what is that to you? Follow me!" So the rumour spread in the community that this disciple would not die. Yet Jesus did not say to him that he would not die, but, "If it is my will that he remain until I come, what is that to you?"

This is the disciple who is testifying to these things and has written them, and we know that his testimony is true. But there are also many other things that Jesus did; if every one of them were written down, I suppose that the world itself could not contain the books that would be written.

Structure

- The risen One appears to some disciples at the Sea of Tiberias (1–14)

  ○ the fishing scene and miracle (1–8)

  ○ the meal on land (9–13)

  ○ the parenthetical observation of the narrator (14)

- The risen One, Peter and the Beloved Disciple (15–24)

  ○ rehabilitation and commissioning (15–17)

  ○ concerning the fate of Peter and the Beloved Disciple (18–24)

- The second solemn Conclusion (25)[7]

Fishing and a Meal

"After these things" is the redactor's attempt to link what follows with the previous Jerusalem narrative. Given the way in which that episode unfolded and concluded, a continuation in a Galilee location is totally unexpected. The opening words state that "Jesus showed himself". This verb (*phaneroō*), to manifest, reveal, is not used to speak of the resurrection appearances in the previous chapter but is used elsewhere in the Fourth Gospel to denote revelation, which takes place through Jesus.[8] This event, therefore, is an epiphany, a revelatory moment.[9]

The storyteller introduces the characters and the contextual situation. Simon Peter decides to go fishing on the Sea of Tiberias, as John prefers to call the Lake of Gennesaret. It looks as if he has returned to his previous means of earning a living, though this was not mentioned earlier, leaving behind his former relationship with Jesus and all that they had experienced together. The death of Jesus has changed everything. He takes the leading role throughout the episode. He is joined in this venture by half a dozen others: Thomas, the 'twin', who featured in the previous story, Nathaniel from Cana, the sons of Zebedee, who have not previously been mentioned,[10] and two who are not named, one of whom presumably is the Beloved Disciple. For these disciples, too, the story of Jesus and their involvement with him are consigned to the past. "The symbolic completeness of the number seven suggests that we are to see the group as representative of the future church community as a whole."[11]

Night was the best time for fishing, and fish could be sold in the morning market.[12] After they have failed to catch anything, and as dawn breaks, (an important symbolic touch recalling 20:1 and the wider darkness and light symbolism), a stranger is present on the shore.[13] It is Jesus, but he goes unrecognised. There is something very different about him; his appearance has been transformed. Addressing them familiarly as "Children" or "Lads" (*paidia*),[14] and aware of their lack of success, he suggests that Simon Peter and his companions should try again on the starboard side of their boat, the lucky side,[15] and assures them of success. They obey his word, and to their surprise make a fine (miraculous!) catch of 153 fish but cannot haul it into the boat because of the amount.[16]

At this miracle, the Beloved Disciple recognises the stranger, and exclaims to Simon Peter, "It is the Lord," the confessional language of Easter faith, recalling Magdalene's message (20:18).[17] Just as in the Empty Tomb story the

Beloved Disciple discerned the significance of the folded cloths, now he is led by the remarkable catch of fish to perceive that it is Jesus on the shore.[18] Peter gets the message, and with typical enthusiasm covers himself quickly, tucks up his outer garment, jumps overboard, and eagerly wades or swims the hundred yards to the nearby shore to reach Jesus, while the others remain in the boat and tow the bulging net to land.[19]

The focus of the narrative changes, as fishing symbolism yields to the symbolism of a meal. For, on reaching land, they discover that Jesus has prepared for them on a charcoal fire a breakfast of bread and fish; the charcoal fire is a reminder of the courtyard of the denials (18:3, 18). Jesus tells them to bring some of the fish they have caught to swell the supplies. Peter, already on shore, springs into action at Jesus' request and boards the boat, presumably getting into the stern to take hold of the net and drag it ashore[20] even though the others were unable to do so earlier.[21] Perhaps his action is symbolic of his leadership, even if the boat belonged to him. The number of the fish, 153, may be factual, but is probably symbolic, indicating perfection, completion, totality.[22] It may prefigure the scope, breadth, universality and magnitude of the catch in the Christian mission. Abundant fish recalls abundant wine at Cana and abundant bread and fish at the earlier banquet near the lake.

The insistence that the nets did not break in spite of the large catch may indicate the evangelist's interest in the unity of the Church; despite the number and variety of its members, the Church remains one and will not be torn apart.[23] The same verb is used in connection with the seamless garment of Jesus (19:23-24); Jesus has spoken of one flock with one shepherd (10:16), and has prayed that the disciples might be one (17:21-23). "The universality of the Christian community, the result of the initiative of Jesus (see v.6), the leadership of the Beloved Disciple and Simon Peter, and the participation of the disciples in the mission, is the main point of the story."[24]

Jesus then invites the group to breakfast. As a result of the faith of the Beloved Disciple and Peter's action, the disciples recognise that it is Jesus who is present, no longer needing to query his identity.[25] Jesus performs the task of the host, taking the bread and giving it to them, and doing the same with the fish.[26] There is no mention of "giving thanks", though some manuscripts provide the phrase. Nevertheless, the resemblance to 6:11, the multiplication of the loaves and fish, the provision of a banquet for thousands in the vicinity of this same lake, is very close. Jesus continues to provide for people after the resurrection as he did before his passion. There is continuity in the relationship,[27] and the eucharistic motif is evident.[28]

Mention of this being the third appearance seems a piece of artificial editing, an attempt to sew the two chapters together. The appearance of Jesus to Magdalene is not included, as the editor is interested in appearances to the group, not to an individual.

Jesus, Simon and the Beloved Disciple

After the conclusion of breakfast, the story continues with a different focus. Jesus addresses Peter as "Simon, son of John", the designation used at their original encounter after Andrew had introduced them and when Jesus changed his name to Cephas, "the Rock".[29] Beside the charcoal fire,[30] which painfully recalls the courtyard of denial, without recrimination or blame, just a gentle allusion, Jesus three times asks Peter whether he loves him. The Greek text is ambiguous. It can mean "more than these disciples love me", or "more than you love anyone and anything else"—everything that has determined his life so far.[31] In the Old Covenant, Israel pledged her unconditional and absolute love for God. Jesus demands of Peter the same loyalty and loving commitment.[32]

Three times the chastened Peter replies: "Yes, Lord, you know I love you".[33] Rather than boast as before, he simply entrusts himself to Jesus' knowledge of his heart without reference to the others.[34] Peter's commitment to love is crucial. Each time Jesus responds to Peter by telling him to feed his flock, and the reader cannot but recall the earlier words of Jesus about the Good Shepherd (10:1–18). Peter's unconditional love is the source of his mission as shepherd of the new community. "There is the sense of past failure being wiped away and swallowed up in present love."[35]

We are meant to understand this episode first as Peter's rehabilitation. The threefold questioning and avowal of love are linked with the threefold denial. Jesus, the shepherd reaching out to his wayward sheep, is affording Peter the opportunity of making up in some way for having let him down so badly, assuring him of his generous forgiveness, measured by the awesome responsibility he subsequently bestows. Secondly, the scene depicts Peter's pastoral commissioning. Some maintain that the threefold repetition of the command to tend the lambs and sheep adds to the obvious solemnity of the occasion. It is significant that Jesus insists on love as a necessary prerequisite for this role, love for him in the first place. Peter must be utterly devoted to his Master; only then can he be entrusted with the care of the flock. Mission flows from relationship. "The threefold profession of love and commitment of the part of Peter therefore reinforces the idea that Peter's unconditional love for Jesus is the foundation and source of his mission as the shepherd of the new covenant community."[36] And the flock for which Peter must care remains the flock of Jesus; the sheep continue to belong to Jesus: "my sheep." Peter does not replace Jesus but has responsibility for keeping the flock safe.[37] Just as Yahweh in the Old Testament delegated his shepherding role to others, so does Jesus in the New.

In the biblical tradition the role of shepherd implies authority.[38] Peter shares in the authority of Jesus. However, in delineating the characteristic traits of the Good Shepherd, John omits all reference to power, status, superiority and prerogatives. He emphasises aspects of pastoral care: knowledge and familiarity, affectionate solicitude and help, protection, and dedication.[39]

The outstanding note of John's portrayal of the Good Shepherd is self-giving, self-sacrifice. Our current text moves naturally to the same theme, as Jesus indicates that Peter will also share his destiny of violent death. During the dialogue at the Supper, Peter boasted that he was ready to lay down his life for Jesus (13:36); subsequent events proved him badly mistaken. Now the risen Lord assures him that he will express his avowed love precisely in this way: "When you were younger, you used to fasten your own belt, and to go wherever you wished. But when you grow old, you will stretch out your hands, and someone else will fasten a belt around you, and take you where you do not wish to go" (21:18).[40] Scholars dispute whether these words imply crucifixion specifically, or simply captivity as a prelude to death. For the evangelist, they clearly indicate that Peter will follow the shepherd pattern of Jesus and glorify God by obediently surrendering to death for the sake of the sheep.

Finally, Jesus adds the injunction "Follow me." At the Supper, when Peter asked Jesus where he was going, he answered: "I am going where you cannot follow me now, but one day you will" (13:36). Peter then asserted his willingness to lay down his life for Jesus, a claim soon discounted. Now Jesus is calling him again, a call to genuine discipleship. Now Peter can follow Jesus, because he is no longer self-confident and is empowered from above. In his case, the discipleship of self-giving service will demand martyrdom, love to the end and the uttermost.[41]

As Peter follows, he turns and catches sight of the disciple whom Jesus loved, who is following them; the Supper is explicitly recalled.[42] He asks Jesus about his fate: "Lord, what about him?"[43] These two disciples have been closely connected in the later part of the Gospel: the final Supper, the courtyard of the high priest, and at the empty tomb. On these earlier occasions the role of Beloved Disciple is the more positive and his behaviour the more impressive. For the Johannine community he was a founding figure and hero.[44] But the risen Jesus has just reconstituted Peter's discipleship and appointed him as pastor of the flock, so the issue for Peter and the reader is where does the Beloved Disciple now stand.

Jesus' reply seems a little sharp! "If it is my will that he remain until I come, what is that to you? Follow me." Peter needs to focus on his own discipleship. It would seem that there was in the Johannine community a tradition of a saying of Jesus whereby the Beloved Disciple would not die before Jesus' return. The narrator is at pains to scotch this rumour, to clarify the resultant misunderstanding. What Jesus really said was "If it is my will that he remain until I come …" "The possibility is contemplated … though not definitely affirmed".[45] "The probable background is that the Johannine community was disturbed by the death of their revered master, since they expected him not to die. Furthermore, if he died of natural causes rather than through martyrdom, the community may have felt a loss of prestige."[46] So the author seeks to ensure that the founding figure of the community has not lost status through his natural death but is equally honoured. Both he and Peter gave glory to God, but in different ways. "Both roles are to be seen as in line with Jesus' sovereign will and as appropriate to discipleship."[47] What is important is the fulfilment of Jesus' will.

> The roles of Peter and the Beloved Disciple can be seen as two models for the continuation of Jesus' mission through the lives of his followers. While the witness of Peter is characterised by his shepherding and his following of Jesus to death, the witness of the Beloved Disciple will be characterised by his foundational role in the passing on of authentic interpretation of the tradition about Jesus in this narrative … Disciples are to be faithful followers in whatever role the risen Lord assigns them.[48]

The narrator then highlights the fact that "this is the disciple who is testifying to these things and has written them, and we know that his testimony is true." In a sense he does "remain", for his authentic and trustworthy testimony is contained in the tradition about the ministry of Jesus, his words and deeds, his death and resurrection, which he has handed down, now written in the book which we call John's Gospel. The community, of which the narrator is a member, expresses their conviction of the authenticity of this writing, and also of their consequent way of living.[49]

This fascinating episode highlights the beginnings of a Christian tradition of great importance. Peter is appointed by Jesus as the shepherd of the flock; his governing, authority and leadership is founded on his love for Jesus; he will carry out this role of self-giving service to the point of death. The Beloved Disciple is essentially the witness who hands on the genuine Jesus tradition, a tradition which continues to our own day through his written word.[50] The two roles are different, but complementary.[51]

Reflections

While this chapter clearly concerns Peter and the Beloved Disciple, and the situation of the Johannine community at the time, there are still lessons that we can learn, indications of ongoing aspects of Christian living applicable to us today.

The Jesus of this story displays the characteristics we have met earlier in the ministry. There is a gentle authority about him as he orchestrates the proceedings. The level of his forgiveness is breathtaking, as he reaches out to Simon Peter and enables him in some way to make up for his failure by the charcoal fire in the high priest's courtyard. He not only forgives him but gives him major responsibility in the community coming into existence through the resurrection. He places his trust in Peter and in his love. I find this very reassuring in my own stumbling life journey. Jesus is so incredibly faithful; nothing can stop him loving us. This links in with the imagery of abundance—a huge catch of fish, just as there were the 120 gallons of top-quality wine at Cana and twelve baskets left over after the feeding of the five thousand. Such abundance reflects the abundance of Jesus' love, and the love of the Father who sent/gave him, love to the uttermost, love without limits. The breakfast meal on the shore reminds us that every time we celebrate the Eucharist centuries later, we encounter this forgiveness and this love, and are caught up in the mystery of it all, "drawn in" more fully into the life of God that we share.[52]

The fishing and shepherd imagery are indications of our call to mission. As disciples we are sent ones, commissioned to draw others into our experience of sharing life with Jesus, which the Synoptics refer to as the Kingdom, the reigning presence of the God of love. We are also commissioned to foster the unity of the community, to overcome whatever is divisive or destructive. All of us are called to make real in our different life situations the shepherding of Jesus as outlined in his famous parable: he knows each sheep by name, seeks out good pasture for them, is protective and caring, seeks to be inclusive, is concerned that the sheep have life to the fullest. This can be demanding and costly; it entails generosity and self-giving; it may even entail a willingness to give one's life.[53]

The Gospel closes with a comment about what has been "written down", and the testimony of the writer and his community that it is true. This is an invitation to us to read attentively and with an open mind and heart whatever has been written for our well-being, our growth in faith, the deepening of our aliveness in Jesus.

Finally, the question that Jesus poses to Simon Peter is addressed also to us: "Do you love me?" "Do you love me more than anyone and anything else?" As we read the love story which is John's Gospel, we become increasingly aware of his love for us, his love *eis telos,* to the end and the uttermost, and this knowledge should enable us to respond positively: "Yes, Lord, you know that I love you." Discipleship has two aspects, exemplified in both Peter and the Beloved Disciple; we are loved unconditionally by Jesus, and we seek to love him. And we are sent to reach out to others in mission, a mission of self-giving and care, and a mission of witness through life and proclaiming the word.

Notes

1   Dunn, *Jesus Remembered,* 854, believes that in this story there are indications of an early reminiscence, uncomplicated by later perspectives.

2   For a detailed treatment see Francis J. Moloney, *Johannine Studies 1975–2017* (Tubingen: Mohr Siebeck, 2017), 522–527. He notes two common threads to

the wide variety of views. There are parallels between the themes and the language used to express them across John 1–20 and John 21; the traditional reading of John 1–20:31 as a literary and theological unity leaves a number of questions unanswered, to which necessary answers are provided in John 21. The elements of continuity which he rehearses on pp. 527–531 show that John 21 has its roots in the Johannine tradition and a deep familiarity with the story as it is told in John 1–20. He engages with elements of discontinuity on pp. 532–535.

3   Culpepper, *Gospel and Letters*, 245.

4   Moloney, *Johannine Studies*, 536; Brown, *John*, 2, 1078, 1083; Moloney, *John*, 545–46; *Resurrection*, 117. On p. 133, n. 53, he asserts that although chapters 20 and 21 were written separately, they are to be read together; Chennattu, *Covenant*, 168, states that the text as it stands in the Gospel is a well-unified narrative. Schneiders, *Written*, 202, sees chapter 21 as an integral part of the Gospel in fundamental theological continuity with chapters 1–20, and that its purpose is to bring the Gospel account to a close by transferring the reader's attention from the experience of the first disciples with the historical Jesus to the experience of the contemporary Church with the glorified Jesus, from the story of those who "saw" to the story of those who "believe without having seen". Lincoln, *John*, 508, stresses that it is an integral part of the final form of the Gospel, and notes that the focus on matters of authority and structure and the role of the Beloved Disciple suggest later reflection on specific issues that have arisen at a late stage of the Gospel's composition.

5   Brown, *John*, 2, 1078–92, who considers that the epilogue balances the initial prologue; the redactor wishes to preserve important material and emphasise specific theological themes; Culpepper, *Gospel and Letters*, 244–45; Byrne, *Life Abounding*, 342. Moloney, *John*, 546, stresses that it belongs to the Gospel as we have it, and is not simply an addendum or postscript, or afterthought.

6   Culpepper, *Gospel and Letters*, 245. Schneiders, *Written*, 202, asks whether this chapter is intended to be a quasi-literal account of a historical event, or essentially a symbolic exploration of the post-resurrection experience of the Johannine community with implications for the Church of all time.

7   Brown, *John*, 2, 1083–84, believes that the arguments in favour of the unity of 1–14 and 15–17 are more persuasive than the arguments against it. On 2, 1094, he speculates that the material in 1–17 may consist of a combination of a first appearance of Jesus to Peter in a fishing scene and the story of the first Galilean appearance to the Twelve at a meal of bread and fish. Many scholars take 24–25 as the conclusion (see Lincoln, *John*, 509; Brown, *John*, 2, 1123; Culpepper, *Gospel and Letters*, 250). Moloney, *John*, 546–47, places 24 with the previous section, following the major characters, leaving 25 alone, as matching 20:30–31; also, *Resurrection*, 118; likewise, Byrne, *Life Abounding*, 344; Barrett, *John*, 480. Schneiders, *Written*, 203, sees 1–14 as basically 2 units: the revelation of Jesus to his disciples and their recognition of him, and the relationship of two central roles in the community of

118

disciples, contemplation and mission, represented by the related activities of the Beloved Disciple and Peter.

8   Moloney, *Resurrection*, 118; see 1:31; 2:11; 3:21; 7:4; 9:3; 17:6. It is rare in the Synoptic tradition and is found for a post-resurrection appearance only in the Markan appendix (16:12, 14); Barrett, *John*, 481; Brown, *John*, 2, 1095.

9   Lincoln, *John*, 510, calls this self-revelation an epiphany. Chennattu, *Covenant*, 169, notes that the sign of the catch of fish needs to be interpreted as a continuation of the revelatory aspect of Jesus' works.

10   These brothers have not previously been named in John. Byrne, *Life Abounding*, 344, notes similarities with the Cana story, as does Lincoln, *John*, 515: the verb "revealed" and the disciples' belief; the presence of Nathaniel, and the greater things promised in 1:51; abundant wine and fish.

11   Byrne, *Life Abounding*, 344; Lincoln, *John*, 510; he notes that Nathaniel was promised that he would see greater things (1:49–50); this is now part of the fulfilment. Also, Chennattu, *Covenant*, 170. Moloney, *John*, 548, observes that the theme of the creation of a new community at the cross (19:25–27) continues. Schneiders, *Written*, 206, sees seven as a symbol of fullness and perfection; the community of fishers is not exclusively the apostolic college, but the complete post-resurrection community of believers who encounter him down through the centuries in the eucharistic meal he prepares.

12   Brown, *John*, 2, 1069; Lindars, *John*, 625.

13   Brown, *John*, 2, 1089–92, provides a detailed comparison between John and Luke 5, concluding that Luke and John have independently preserved variant forms of the same miracle story; these forms probably derive from a single post-Easter appearance of Jesus to Peter in Galilee; Byrne, *Life Abounding*, 345, n. 57; Culpepper, *Gospel and Letters*, 246, suggests a common tradition lies behind Luke 15 and John 21; similarly, Schneiders, *Written*, 204. Lincoln, *John*, 514–15, discusses at length the relationship between John and Luke; he believes that John was aware of Luke; also Schneiders, *Jesus Risen*, 48. Koester, *Symbolism*, 135, notes that the connection between fishing and missionary activity is almost proverbial in the Synoptic Gospels, which suggests that it was widely known in Christian circles.

14   Moloney, *John*, 549; *Resurrection*, 119, refers to "an intimate authority". Though not found elsewhere in the Gospel, it is found in 1 John (2:14, 18; 3:7), and has the sense of someone treasured, as a parent treasures a child. Brown, *John*, 2, 1070, senses a colloquial touch, and prefers "my boys" or "lads." He notes that never in the Gospels do the disciples catch fish without Jesus' help. Culpepper, *Gospel and Letters*, 246, sees the term of endearment as important in view of John's development of the theme of disciples as "children of God" (1:12).

15   The right side was the auspicious or lucky side; but the writer was not entertaining the possibility of luck! A miracle was about to take place. See Brown, *John*, 2, 1071; Barrett, *John*, 482.

16   The verb *helkein* or *helkyein* is used of people being drawn to Jesus by the Father (6:44) or when he is "lifted up" (12:32). Fishing is a symbol of the disciples' apostolic mission. Lincoln, *John*, 511, links the large number of fish with Ezek 47:10 LXX and Jesus as the new temple.

17   The two disciples prominent in the story about the empty tomb take central roles in this narrative too. Barrett, *John*, 480, comments that Peter is the quicker to act, the Beloved Disciple the quicker to see and believe. Schneiders, *Written*, 203, describes the Beloved Disciple as the "privileged locus of and witness to God's self-revelation in Jesus." On p.205, she sees the Beloved Disciple as the Fourth Gospel's "paradigmatic embodiment of contemplative openness to the revelation of Jesus." He recognises Jesus first and proclaims him authoritatively. Peter responds, and this grounds his pastoral leadership. Brown, *John*, 2, 1096, believes that in the original story it was probably Peter who recognised Jesus, "but this honour now belongs to the Beloved Disciple, who, because his is closely bound to Jesus by love, is best attuned to recognise him."

18   Moloney, *John*, 550, notes that whereas in chapter 20 the Beloved Disciple believes without seeing, now he believes because he sees Jesus.

19   The idea seems to be that Peter was lightly clad while fishing; he could not remove the garment to go swimming, for that would leave him naked, which was not acceptable when greeting someone, so he tucks in his outer garment. Or, wearing only a fisherman's smock, he tucks it into his belt. He swims rather than wades, for the shoreline drops off rapidly; Brown, *John*, 2, 1072; Moloney, *Resurrection*, 134, n. 56. The verb is found in 13:4-5, when Jesus girds himself with the towel, and nowhere else in the New Testament. Lincoln, *John*, 512, however, thinks it was common to be naked when fishing, so Peter is getting dressed before meeting Jesus. Schneiders, *Written*, 203, suggests that Peter's coming to Jesus through water could evoke baptismal images (3:5). Koester, *Symbolism*, 137, sees Peter's hurling himself into the water as an act of devotion; his care to remain clothed was a religious act.

20   The verb which is twice used for hauling or dragging the net is '*helkein*' or '*helkyein*' (21:6, 11). For Koester, *Symbolism*, 134, this is the core action of this part of the story. Jesus uses the same term in the discourse on the bread of life when he says: "No one can come to me unless drawn by the Father who sent me; and I will raise that person up on the last day" (6:44). This shows that human beings cannot generate their own faith; they are dependent on God's action. Later, in a passion prediction, Jesus says: "And I, when I am lifted up from the earth, will draw all people to myself" (12:32); Jesus does the drawing. Koester, *Word of Life*, 130; *Symbolism*, 135, notes that Jesus, the missionary, now does this through the work of the disciples.

21 For Chennattu, *Covenant*, 171, the abundance motif brings home the presence of the messianic era and signals the actualisation of the new messianic covenant community. Byrne, *Life Abounding*, 346, suggests that Jesus' using his fish and theirs indicates continuity of their mission with his. Moloney, *John*, 550, notes how Peter's presence links the miraculous haul of fish with the meal. Whatever their prehistory, the two are skilfully joined.

22 Byrne, *Life Abounding*, 347. Many suggestions have been made to explain this number; for a detailed treatment see Lindars, *John*, 629–31; Brown, *John*, 2, 1074–76, who concludes that the origin of the number probably lies in the direction of an emphasis on the authentic eyewitness character of what has been recorded. The number would have been retained in the story because it was so large; and when the account received a symbolic interpretation, the number would have been interpreted as a figurative indication of the magnitude of the results of the disciples' mission; this interpretation is not a solution to the problem of historicity. Byrne, *Life Abounding*, 347, n. 63, recalls Augustine's suggestion that 153 is the sum of the numbers 1–17; 17 is the sum of 7 and 10, both of which separately indicate perfection and completeness. Another view is that the number of species of fish known at the time was 153. Lincoln, *John*, 512, refers to the completeness and unity of those drawn in by the disciples' mission, and Barrett, *John*, 484, to completeness and perfection; Chennattu, *Covenant*, 172, suggests the "all-embracing or universal character of the mission making disciples of every race on the earth." For Schneiders, *Written*, 204, the enormous catch, possible only at Jesus' command, represents the universal mission of the Church carried out by those who without Jesus can do nothing (see 15:5, but who will be fruitful as long as they abide in him and obey his commands.) As Moloney, *Resurrection*, 120, states: "The never-ending proposals for its meaning probably indicate that, whatever its meaning, it is lost to us now."

23 Brown, *John*, 2, 1097; Schneiders, *Written*, 204, who notes that unity is the primary theme in Jesus' Supper prayer (17:20–21); by the time the Gospel was written it was a problem in the Johannine community, as the epistles illustrate. For Koester, *Symbolism*, 135, "this interpretation is at most an interesting possibility."

24 Moloney, *Resurrection*, 120; Byrne, *Life Abounding*, 346. Brown, *John*, 2, 1098, notes that the appearance story (1–14) lacks words of commission; the lack is only partially fulfilled in Jesus' words to Peter in 15–17; he sees the catch of fish as a dramatic equivalent of the command of Jesus in Matt 28:19.

25 Lindars, *John*, 631, states that they need not ask a question because they know the answer.

26 Lincoln, *John*, 513, suggests that it is Jesus' hosting of the meal which leads to the other disciples recognising who he is (as Luke 24:30–31). In 16:23 Jesus says that his disciples will not question him about anything. Schneiders, *Written*, 204, also maintains that the other disciples recognise Jesus in the sharing of the

meal. Chennattu, *Covenant,* 174, notes that a shared meal plays a significant role in deepening a friendship bond and the commitment to one another within the context of making a covenant.

27   Koester, *Symbolism,* 136.

28   Byrne, *Life Abounding,* 347; Lincoln, *John,* 514; Brown, *John,* 2, 1077, 1099; Culpepper, *Gospel and Letters,* 247. Moloney, *Resurrection,* 121, notes that the eucharistic hints indicate the presence of one of the central acts of worship of the Johannine community. Barrett, *John,* 484, says "this meal was probably intended to call to the minds of the readers eucharistic associations."

29   1:41–42. Brown, *John,* 2, 1102, suggests that Jesus may be treating him less familiarly, and thus challenging his friendship. Koester, *Symbolism,* 136, observes that the leadership of Peter was evident in the earlier part of the story; his leadership position is now reaffirmed through shepherd imagery.

30   *anthrakia,* as in 18:18, 25.

31   Moloney, *John,* 559, 554, believes that the more likely comparison is between Peter's love of his disciples and his love for Jesus; in *Resurrection,* 121, he suggests it refers to "everything that has determined his life to this point: boats, nets, the catch, or anything else that might be self-serving." Byrne, *Life Abounding,* 348, n. 67, maintains that the "these" must refer to the other disciples; similarly, Lincoln, *John,* 517; Lindars, *John,* 635. Brown,*John,* 2, 1104, suggests that the comparative clause is not important, since Peter's answer does not allude to it. Culpepper, *Gospel and Letters,* 248, is open to both possibilities.

32   Chennattu, *Covenant,* 174–5. Brown, *John,* 2, 1115, speaks of a love of total attachment and exclusive service.

33   The evangelist varies his verbs for "love" in Jesus' questions and Peter's replies (*agapan, philein*); most scholars consider the variations to be purely stylistic; the same is true for the verbs for "feed" (*boskein, poimanein*) and the nouns for sheep (*arnia, probata*). Brown, *John,* 2, 1103; Byrne, *Life Abounding,* 350; Moloney, *John,* 559; *Resurrection,* 135, n.64; Lincoln, *John,* 517; Barrett, *John,* 486.

34   Lincoln, *John,* 517, notes the poignancy of Peter's appeal to Jesus' sovereign knowledge, given that his denials had been predicted. Brown, *John,* 2, 1106, observes that while Peter is hurt because he has been asked three times, some trace his sorrow also to the fact that by his denials he had given Jesus cause to doubt him.

35   Byrne, *Life Abounding,* 348. Brown, *John,* 2, 1088–9, considers that the post-resurrectional period was the original setting for Matt 16:18–19a. "The two sayings are not close enough to be doublets, but they represent fragments of a longer original narrative of a post-resurrection appearance to Peter wherein he was given authority in the early church."

36   Chennattu, *Covenant*, 178.

37   Lincoln, *John*, 518, writes that Peter is charged with the privilege and responsibility of being the undershepherd who will protect, nourish and tend the flock of the Good Shepherd himself.

38   1 Chron 17:6; 2 Sam 5:2. See Brown, *John*, 2, 1114; in the Old Testament, Israel's leaders share in God's authority as God's delegates. For an excellent treatment of the shepherding theme, see Kenneth E. Bailey, *The Good Shepherd* (London: SPCK, 2015).

39   10:1–30. See also 1 Peter 5:1–4. As Byrne, *Life Abounding*, 349–50, observes, interpreters tend to divide along denominational lines when assessing the authority accorded to Peter here. Peter is being singled out and given an authoritative commission. It is significant that the Johannine author felt it important some years after Peter's death to remind the community of the pastoral authority given to him by the Lord. "That Peter is presented in this way suggests that the authority conferred upon him continues in the community in some significant way."

40   Koester, *Symbolism*, 137, notes that when in the boat, Peter had girded himself before jumping overboard to reach Jesus, now others will gird him. Moloney, *John*, 559, links Peter's youth with his relationship with Jesus prior to Jesus' death and resurrection, full of vigour and confidence, contrasted with his subsequent experience, the fruit of his unconditional love.

41   See 13:1; 12:26. By the time the Gospel was written, Peter had been martyred. The text reads "the kind of death by which he would glorify God", a phrase used of Jesus in 12:33; 18:32; see also 11:4; 12:27–28; 13:31–32.

42   He follows physically, but his following entails lifelong, undeviating discipleship (Moloney, *John*, 556).

43   Moloney, *John*, 560, notes that Peter asks a question which gives the author space to have Jesus ease the anxiety that may have been generated by the Beloved Disciple's death; in *Resurrection*, 124, he states that a post-Easter Johannine community of "followers", aware that they have all been commanded to love as Jesus has loved, look back upon these two foundational figures and ask about the relative significance of their roles in the ongoing life of love to which they have been called. Brown, *John*, 2, 1118, thinks that two independent sayings (vv. 18 and 22) transmitted in the Johannine tradition have been joined together and added to the post-resurrection narrative.

44   Byrne, *Life Abounding*, 351; Moloney, *Resurrection*, 124.

45   Barrett, *John*, 488. He comments that the earliest Christians believed that the parousia would occur before the first generation of Christians disappeared (Mark 9:1).

46   Byrne, *Life Abounding*, 352; Lincoln, *John*, 521, who also notes the undermining effect of a prediction of Jesus proving unreliable. The credibility of Jesus

has been an issue. Brown, *John*, 2, 1118, notes that for the Johannine community the Beloved Disciple seems to have been the last of the apostolic generation.

47   Lincoln, *John*, 520.

48   Lincoln, *John*, 522. Barrett, *John*, 485–86, states that though the Beloved Disciple was not a witness (*martys*) in the same way as Peter, he was a witness (*martys*), and was responsible for the witness (*martyria*) contained in the Gospel itself, and through the written Gospel he constitutes himself the permanent guarantor of the Church's tradition.

49   Byrne, *Life Abounding*, 353, reminds us that the Beloved Disciple may not himself have actually committed his testimony to writing, but is the author of the text in that he "instigated its composition as a record of his unique witness to the life-giving revelation disclosed in Jesus." Similarly, Lincoln, *John*, 523, who adds that "the Beloved Disciple is being claimed as the authority for the distinctive perspective that has shaped and pervaded the witness of the narrative." Brown, *John*, 2, 1125, believes that the "we" refers to the Johannine writer responsible for the addition of chapter 21 and his fellow Johannine disciples, assuring the readers that the new work was no less authoritative than the old and that the whole stemmed from the Beloved Disciple whose witness was true. Lindars, *John*, 641, states that the "we" represents the *imprimatur* of the Church in which it originated. Moloney, *John*, 562, suggests that in many ways the "we" involves generations of Christian readers who know that this witness is true and who can give witness to their own belief that the truth sets people free. Koester, *Symbolism*, 138, notes that despite the reality of his death, the disciple would continue to witness through the testimony preserved in the Gospel, and his witness would remain vital to the church's mission.

50   See Moloney, *Resurrection*, 126; Byrne, *Life Abounding*, 354. Lincoln, *John*, 524, adds that the writing down of the narrative itself and the Beloved Disciple's witness that it represents play an integral role in the continuation of Jesus' mission within history. Brown, *John*, 2, 1129, observes that the Johannine notion of true witness goes beyond an eyewitness report of what happened; it includes the adaptation of what happened so that its truth can be seen by and be significant for subsequent generations.

51   Barrett, *John*, 480, states that the two are represented as partners, of whom neither can take precedence over the other. "Peter is the head of the evangelistic and pastoral work of the Church, but the beloved disciple is the guarantor of its tradition regarding Jesus."

52   For a deep and inspiring treatment of the theme of love in the Fourth Gospel, see Moloney, *Love in the Gospel of John*.

53   I have explored this theme in *Symbols and Spirituality. Reflecting on John's Gospel* (Bolton: Don Bosco Publications, 2007), 80–93; see also David O'Malley, *The Christian Teacher. Shepherd of Loving Kindness* (Bolton: Don Bosco Publications, 2007).

Concluding Thoughts

In this final chapter, by way of conclusion, I would like to treat two topics. The first concerns some issues of a historical nature. The second explores the meaning of being "Alive".

Some Historical Issues

In the introduction I referred to the three dimensions of our approach to scriptural texts: theological, literary and historical. Throughout this book I have concentrated on attempting to elucidate what God is saying to us (the *logos tou theou*), what is the message of these stories, what they reveal about Jesus and how they challenge our discipleship and engage our spirituality. In the process I have often made comments of a literary nature, highlighting elements like structure, irony and suspense. Issues of a historical nature have usually been relegated to this chapter. Our focus throughout has been the events at the tomb and the appearances of Jesus, both of which give rise to historical questions. Naturally, we are keen to know what really happened.[1]

Our liturgical celebration of Easter Sunday, on "the third day",[2] suggests that the situation of desolation, utter crisis and emptiness, which the friends of Jesus must have felt after his death and burial, did not last long, less than forty-eight hours, in fact. Each Gospel relates a story of women visiting the tomb when the Sabbath was over and finding it empty.[3] Luke describes appearances of Jesus to the disciples on their way to Emmaus and then to a larger group; his account of Easter is compressed into that one day, the culmination of Jesus' "exodus".[4] And John, too, has Jesus appear to the disciples on that day. Events at the tomb may well have occurred on that day, but this is probably not the case historically with the appearances.

An explicit reference to the empty tomb is not found in the early Christian hymns, formulas or confessions, or in the writings of Paul.[5] Each of the Gospels does contain an account of its discovery but comparing the various versions can be perplexing. There are discrepancies with regard to the time, the names of the women, their purpose in going to the tomb, the visual phenomena that occur, the conversation and the reactions.[6] The earliest tradition about that Sunday morning is probably found in John, where Magdalene goes to the tomb, finds the stone removed,[7] but no Jesus.[8] In the other Gospels other women accompany her. She departs to inform the disciples that the tomb is empty, suggesting that people have removed the body. That Jesus should have been raised to life does not occur to her. The empty tomb does not give rise to resurrection faith; it is not a 'proof' of the resurrection.[9]

The key factor in the Synoptic accounts is the appearance of an angel or angelic young men who, with different wording, interpret the empty tomb and proclaim the Easter kerygma.[10] While most Christian scholars accept the historicity of the discovery of the empty tomb,[11] they believe that the angelic visitor(s) and message are not factual but a later addition to the basic story, providing an explanation for the empty tomb tradition. This is a classic biblical technique. It transforms the tradition so as to create a vehicle for the proclamation of Easter faith.[12] The reason for the emptiness of the tomb becomes part of the narrative.[13]

It is the view of many scholars that, in all probability, most of the disciples fled Jerusalem and hot-footed it back to their Galilee homeland.[14] Some of them had probably done so as early as Thursday evening, the rest after the Passover Sabbath. News of an empty tomb, had they heard it, would have increased their confusion and fright. In his wonderful Emmaus narrative, Luke captures, I think, their near despair and shattered dreams: "We had hoped that he was the one to redeem Israel." The disciples returned to Galilee in utter crisis, as confused, broken and disillusioned people; life's new meaning had evaporated. It was also safer for them there. They may have resumed their former occupations.[15] Probably some followers and sympathisers remained in Jerusalem; perhaps their families were residents there. Mary Magdalene and some other women did remain in the city initially; tradition suggests that Jesus appeared to them there.[16] But this seems not to have made an impact on the male disciples when they heard about it at the time or later in Galilee.

But soon, something decisive happened back in Galilee to change it all. There are unexpected, out of the blue encounters or meetings between Jesus and

Peter,[17] Jesus and a group of the others. Fearful, disillusioned, heartbroken people were suddenly transformed; there was a complete turnaround. Maybe these meetings, these experiences, happened at a meal or by the lake, or both; but it is these encounters which gave birth to faith in the resurrection of Jesus, the belief that he was alive.[18] The way the disciples later described what had happened was to claim that Jesus "appeared" to them (or "let himself be seen by them"); there seems to be some kind of visual component.[19] They recognised him. The initiative was with Jesus; the experiences were God's gift, God breaking into their lives again. Possibly, the risen Lord poured out the Spirit on them at that time and commissioned them. These encounters also explained why the tomb was empty, why it had been pointless and misguided to seek the living among the dead (Luke 24:5).

It would seem that for the feast of Pentecost, if not before, the disciples, family and friends of Jesus returned with other pilgrims to Jerusalem for the celebration.[20] Their fear and confusion dissipated, they joined the disciples who had remained. They were convinced that Jesus was alive, and that God had raised him. While they were there something else happened: the presence of the Spirit of God was charismatically manifested.[21] The first community came to be established and was centred in Jerusalem. Filled with the Spirit, the disciples began to go out with great courage and tell people with deep conviction that the Jesus whom their leaders had had killed by the Romans was alive; God had vindicated Jesus' trusting surrender, his self-giving in love, by raising him from death; therefore, God really was behind his message and values and lifestyle and Kingdom dream. They were convinced that with the resurrection of Jesus the last days had arrived, the new age had been inaugurated, the final phase of God's interaction with the world.[22]

Initially, as we have seen in the Introduction, simple phrases and short kerygmatic formulas were used to articulate their deep faith conviction. As well as in the letters of Paul, there are good examples of these early formulas in Peter's five early sermons in Acts.[23] Decades later the evangelists proclaimed their resurrection faith in the form of narratives, and these we have carefully considered. The danger for a contemporary reader is to believe that these stories contain detailed biographical information or are reconstructions of the events. In reality they are catechetical stories. In narrating the same basic appearance of Jesus to the group of disciples, each evangelist is creatively pursuing his own theological purpose and pastoral sensitivity, exploring the meaning of the resurrection of Jesus for Jesus himself and its implications for the Christian communities to which they belonged.[24]

Clearly, the language of resurrection does not mean that Jesus came back to life as it was before (like Jairus' daughter, Lazarus or the son of the widow of Nain); it does not refer to the reanimation of a corpse. It means that Jesus moved forward into a radically new and very different kind of life, beyond all the limitations of space and time. In a variety of ways the evangelists stress that there is continuity—it is the same Jesus as walked the paths of Galilee; but there is an immense difference and transformation, a completely new dimension.[25] Jesus has been freed from death and from all that holds back humanity's growth towards God, and is now actively present in the world.[26] Benedict XVI comments that Jesus breaks into an entirely new form of life, a life which opens up a new dimension of human existence; it is an evolutionary leap.[27] According to the Jewish way of thinking, 'body' denotes the whole person, not simply the physical or material aspect; it was not possible to imagine the risen Jesus without a body. "But naturally they are not thinking of a physical, flesh and blood body, subject to the power of death; rather, it is a 'glorious' body that expresses and gives fullness to the real life he lived in the world."[28] The early Christians understand Jesus' resurrection as a creative action of God, an expression of God's power, which draws him into God's own life; it therefore transcends anything we can experience or describe.[29]

The early formula in Paul's letter to the community in Corinth introduced the language of "appearing": "he appeared to Cephas, then to the twelve." In the Gospel narratives, as well as "appeared" or "showed himself", where the emphasis is on the action of Jesus, we more frequently come across the verb "see".[30] There is also the language of communication, speaking and hearing. It is clear that there was an encounter between the risen Jesus and the disciples, and there was communication.[31] But there is a danger that we interpret this terminology literally, forgetting that our human language, fashioned in space and time, breaks down when attempting to describe what is simply far beyond the scope of human categories, and completely outside our normal frame of reference. It can only be a pale approximation, totally inadequate.

One key element of the narratives is Jesus' commissioning of his disciples. The wording is different in each Gospel, reflecting the style of the individual evangelist. The writers articulate and put into the mouth of Jesus what over the years they have come to understand is entailed by the Christian mission.[32] Something indescribable took place; the recipients of the experience were convinced that Jesus was alive and glorified, that he loved them still and forgave them, and that he entrusted them with a mission. Through their witness the Church came into existence, and we accept that witness.[33]

Another difficult concept, which is clearly fundamental, is that of bodily resurrection. The Lukan Jesus makes it clear that he is not a ghost: "Look at my hands and my feet; see that it is I myself. Touch me and see; for a ghost does not have flesh and bones as you see that I have". He shows them his hands and feet, and even asks for something to eat to prove it (24:39–43). In John, Jesus invites Thomas to "put your finger here and see my hands. Reach out your hand and put it in my side" (20:27). The bodily aspect, the sameness and corporeal continuity of Jesus is emphasised in this way. Paul himself believes that Jesus rose bodily from the dead but rejects the idea that the risen body was physical or natural.[34] Later in the first letter to the Corinthians, he emphasises the transformation involved in resurrection, the otherness of Jesus; he refers to a spiritual body, a glorified body. This he likens to a kernel of grain sown in the ground and the wheat which emerges.[35]

Brown concludes his study with a quotation from Pope Paul VI:

> Jesus rose again in the same body he had taken from the Blessed Virgin, but in new conditions, vivified by a new and immortal animation, which imposes on Christ's flesh the laws and energies of the Spirit. … This new reality … is so far above our capacities of knowledge and even of imagination, that it is necessary to make room for it in our minds through faith.[36]

On Being Alive

The quotation that I used at the beginning of the book was "Because I am alive, you also shall be alive."[37] The immediate effect of the appearance of the risen Jesus to his disciples was that they realised that he was alive and present to them, alive and present in a very different way, but genuinely alive and present. Death had not won; all that he had stood for and passionately sought to establish was not destroyed on Calvary's hill. They understood that this aliveness meant that he was glorified in God's presence; God was behind all that had happened. Quickly they came to see that this meant that he was Messiah[38] and Lord[39] and Saviour. His aliveness brought them alive again, their anguish dissipated, their failure forgiven. Enlightened and empowered by the Spirit, they knew that they just had to share all this with others, that they had a mission to fulfil. Their witness and preaching brought many others to life too, as the new Christian community came to birth.[40] They understood that Jesus was "the firstborn from the dead" (Col 1:18), the first one born into the definitive life of God, and that this is a guarantee and pledge for us and for our world.[41] Our aliveness flows from his being alive.

From the narratives which we have considered it seems that for Mark, our being alive would include overcoming our fears, especially the kind of fear which prevents us from proclaiming the Good News of Jesus' resurrection, and from accepting his servant, self-giving lifestyle and making it our own. For Matthew, as people baptised, we are sent on mission, and we seek to live in accordance with what Jesus has taught, sharing his values and ideals, aware that he is always by our side as our Emmanuel. For Luke, too, to be alive means to be engaged in mission, knowing that we are forgiven people, proclaiming that forgiveness to others. We are sensitive to the word of God in the scriptures, and we celebrate Eucharist together.

In John's Gospel, after his word about aliveness, Jesus continues: "On that day you will know that I am in my Father, and you in me, and I in you." (14:20) The disciples' understanding of the amazing depths of their new aliveness developed over the years, as does ours today. Aliveness means being caught up in the relationship between Father and Son, able to call God "Abba, Father", abiding in the risen Jesus as he abides in us, sharing the very life of God, now in the present, assured that it will continue beyond the grave. This gives a new dimension to every aspect of our existence. Empowered by the Spirit, we are sent to announce in words and by the quality of our love that we have seen the Lord. We do so as members of the New Covenant community, the household of God.

Apart from the Gospel texts, how does all this translate into daily life? What does it mean to be alive? I believe that there are two essential elements to aliveness: awareness and responsiveness.[42] Have I still got a capacity to notice and to wonder, as little children do? How aware, really aware, am I of other people in their unique individuality and diversity, from those close to me in family, community and ministry, to those I meet casually in the street, the supermarket, the train, wherever? How aware am I of the beauty of our natural world in its amazing colour and abundance, shape and texture? How aware am I of our world's tragedy, its greed and untruth, its violence, oppression and injustice, its pain and sadness, what Virgil calls "the tears of things" (*lacrimae rerum*)[43] How aware am I of my own personal reality, what is really going on within me? How aware am I of my responsibility for society, locally, nationally and worldwide, and for our environment? And how aware am I of the presence of Jesus within me, and of the God "in whom I live and move and have my being?" (Acts 17:28).

Since it demands great courage to remain fully exposed and receptive towards these different aspects of our human experience and the God beyond and within it all, since awareness can hurt, we can grow protective shells around ourselves and become a little blind, a little deaf, a little dead. There is, I feel, a lot of deadness around, a lot of apathy. And this can be true of us as individuals, it can be true of families and of institutions, be they religious, educational, social or political. So often we avoid having to respond by fostering a lack of awareness, ways of not seeing, of not hearing. And when we do manage to be aware, we can avoid responding as love would demand.[44] Being half alive, or half dead, can be more comfortable, less stressful. And we can create analgesics for ourselves, subtle strategies of evasion; often we may be doing this unwittingly. The invitation of Moses to the people gathered before him near Shechem can be extended to us too: "Today I offer you the choice of life and death, blessing or curse. Choose life" (Deut 30:19). When speaking about his shepherding role, Jesus is quoted as having said: "I came that they may have life and have it abundantly." Jesus, too, would wish us to choose to be fully alive, aware and generously responsive.

John Taylor writes: "It has long been my conviction that God is not hugely concerned as to whether we are religious or not. What matters to God, and matters supremely, is whether we are alive or not. If your religion brings you more fully to life, God will be in it; but if your religion limits your capacity for life or makes you run away from it, you may be sure that God is against it, just as Jesus was."[45]

Some years ago, I attended a Russell Watson concert in Newcastle upon Tyne; he was my favourite tenor, a local boy made good. He introduced as a guest a young woman from New Zealand, Hayley Westenra, who sang a beautiful, traditional Maori farewell song. Some time later, wishing to sing it myself, I searched for a translation on the Internet, but wasn't successful, so I wrote my own words, and entitled my version 'I've Heard the Music'. These few verses express something of what aliveness has meant for me:

I have wandered in the mountains, in the sunshine and the rain,
I have climbed on rocks and headlands, and the peace has soothed my pain.
I've heard the music of the ice-cold rushing stream,
I have glimpsed the rhythm of my life's unfolding dream.
I have walked along the shoreline, felt my feet sink in the sand.
I have gazed across the water with a pebble in my hand.
I've heard the music of the gentle, whispering breeze.

I have caught the wind's force, felt the breathing of the seas.
I have marvelled at the sunset, shapes and colours in the sky.
I have known the kiss of snowflakes, watched the springtime swallows fly.
I've heard the music of the moon and stars at night.
I have smelled the meadows in the misty, morning light.
I have known the thrill of friendship, coped with grief and spilling tears.
I have loved so many people whose lives touched mine through the years.
I've heard the music of thanksgiving in my heart;
I can welcome life's end now, when it's time for us to part.

For the front cover of this book I chose a photo of the lower reaches of Sourmilk Gill waterfall, as it spills down from Easedale Tarn to the village of Grasmere in the English Lake District, because it evokes the symbolism of living water, so central a theme for the Fourth Evangelist. Jesus speaks about this kind of water to the Samaritan woman by the well of Sychar, water which will quench all our thirsting and become a spring within us, "gushing up to eternal life" (4:10–14). Later, on the final day of the feast of Tabernacles, Jesus, standing in the Jerusalem temple, cries out: "Let anyone who is thirsty come to me, and let the one who believes in me drink." The evangelist continues: "As the scripture has said: 'Out of his heart shall flow streams of living water.' Now he said this about the Spirit, which believers in him were to receive; for as yet there was no Spirit, because Jesus was not yet glorified" (John 7:37–39). Because Jesus has been glorified and is alive, we, too, through the gift of the Spirit, have been brought alive in a new way. The water issuing from his pierced side and open heart on Calvary (19:34) symbolises that new life of the Spirit which he shares with us; and we, alive in him, can be sources of aliveness for others.[46] And so, who wouldn't be alive?

Notes

1   For an excellent, careful and extended treatment of the historical issues, see Moloney, *Resurrection*, 137–148; see also O'Collins, *Easter Jesus*, 3–62; Dunn, *Jesus Remembered*, 825–879.

2   'The third day' means the decisive day; in Hosea, it denotes 'soon'. For

some scholars, the Jewish view was that a person was really dead after the third day, so it means God raised Jesus from real death; see Pagola, *Jesus*, 390. For Lohfink, *Jesus of Nazareth*, 299, the dating stems from events which took place at the tomb.

3   There is no claim in the Gospels or Paul that the resurrection itself was witnessed.

4   In Luke, Jesus ascends on Easter Sunday night after the appearance to the group (24:50–51); he later describes an ascension in Acts (1:6–10). Lohfink, *Jesus of Nazareth*, 290, maintains that Luke has a clear theological motive: "Jerusalem is a symbol of continuity between the time of Jesus and the time of the Church." In John, after the Thomas appearance, the Gospel ends. There is no room in these accounts for Galilee appearances. (Brown, *Bodily Resurrection*, 102).

5   Pagola, *Jesus*, 403; it did not play a significant role in the birth of faith. The very early tradition which Paul uses in writing to the Corinthians (15:3–8) does not explicitly mention the empty tomb; but reference to burial, being raised and appearing, implies an empty tomb tradition. O'Collins, *Easter Jesus*, 44, observes that "for Paul to assert that God raised Jesus from the dead necessarily implies a passage from the tomb." Dodd, *Founder*, 172, states that when the early Christians claimed that Jesus was raised from the dead, they took it for granted that his body was no longer in the tomb.

6   For details, see Brown, *Bodily Resurrection*, 118. Dunn, *Jesus Remembered*, 831, maintains that while Luke and Matthew had access to Mark's version, there were probably various versions in circulation, retellings of the core tradition with variation of detail and embellishments of emphasis. In their churches the story of the empty tomb had no doubt been part of their common tradition, probably as long as their churches had been in existence.

7   Brown, *Bodily Resurrection*, 121, n. 203, notes that the reference to the stone being rolled away may be ancient (it is not mentioned in the burial accounts of Luke and John).

8   Brown, *Bodily Resurrection*, 120. Moloney, *Resurrection*, 145, sees this as the oldest tradition. In the other Gospels, other women accompany Magdalene. In that culture, anyone creating a story would not have placed women as the main protagonists, for their witness was considered without value. Lohfink, *Jesus of Nazareth*, 299, notes elements that suggest a real event. Female witnesses argue in favour of plausibility; polemical opposition presupposes that the tomb was empty. Brown, *Bodily Resurrection*, 126, points out that it would have been impossible for the disciples to preach that God has raised Jesus if the tomb was not empty. He believes it reasonably certain that if the tomb was known, it was empty. The tradition was much older than the subsequent narratives. Dunn, *Jesus Remembered*, 829, believes that a stable core is clear; there is stability within the diverse retellings of the basic core. On p.832, he suggests that the tradition must have emerged from those involved in the episode, "those who in speaking of what they had thus seen

and heard gave the tradition its definitive and lasting shape." One of the firmest features of the tradition in all its variations is the preeminent role attributed to Mary Magdalene and other women. On p.833, he notes that a woman's testimony was discounted in court; such testimony would not have been attributed, especially to Magdalene (formerly demon-possessed—Luke 8:2), unless it was remembered as being the case. Dodd, *Founder,* 173, concludes that the general tradition preserved a genuine memory that on that Sunday morning his tomb was found broken open and, to all appearance, empty. The evangelists seem to have had on their hands a solid piece of tradition, which they were bound to respect because it came down to them from the first witnesses.

9   There is also a tradition that Peter then went to the tomb, in John he was accompanied by the Beloved Disciple (20:3–10), in Luke he was alone (24:10–12), though a later comment suggests that others went too (24:24). Dunn, *Jesus Remembered,* 834–838, notes that the distinctive Jewish burial practice of secondary burial was developed with a view to the hoped-for bodily resurrection. Any claim that a body had been raised would most likely be understood in terms of restoration or reconstitution of the dead body. Physical resurrection necessarily implied empty tomb. There is no hint of an undisturbed burial location. Opponents did not deny that the tomb was empty. Nothing would have so punctured the claims made by Peter and the others than a counter-testimony as to what had happened to Jesus' body—whether undisturbed after proper burial, decomposed beyond recognition or otherwise disposed of. Further, there is no record in the early decades of Christianity of any tomb being venerated as the place where Jesus had been laid to rest. Within contemporary Judaism, the desire to honour the memory of revered dead by constructing appropriate tombs is well attested. Christians did not follow this tradition because they did not believe that any tomb contained his body.

10   A young man in Mark, sitting inside the tomb on the right; an angel in Matthew seated outside on the rolled-back stone; two men in Luke, standing inside; two angels in John, seated inside; these ask a question but give no message. Brown, *Bodily Resurrection,* 122, observes that angelic interpreters were no more than mouthpieces of revelation, without any personality. On p.123, he recognises that the evangelists were aware that they were not dealing with controllable historical facts but with imaginative description. Marshall, *Luke,* 883, considers the angelic message "a literary device" to bring out the significance of the discovery of the empty tomb.

11   Moloney, *Resurrection,* 144; Lohfink, *Jesus of Nazareth,* 299. Schneiders, *Written,* 181, states that "it is probably historically accurate that the tomb of Jesus was found empty on Easter morning; this phenomenon remained ambiguous until it was interpreted by the angel(s), whose words were a reading back into the tomb discovery accounts of what was first revealed by the appearances of the Risen Jesus." It was "after the disciples had come to believe, on the basis of the appearances, that Jesus was risen from the dead, that the empty tomb took on theological and apologetic value as a historical trace of an eschatological event." In *Jesus Risen,*

15–18, she notes that any proclamation of resurrection would have been discredited by Jews and Romans if the tomb was not empty. If the story were invented, women would not have been chosen as main protagonists, since their witness had no value. The literary evidence is unanimous. See also O'Collins, *Easter Jesus*, 38–43.

12   Brown, *Bodily Resurrection*, 121–22, to develop a narrative of the empty tomb to pass on, an explanation had to be included; the style of apocalyptic literature suggested the way to do this; the explanation is thus woven into the narrative.

13   Brown, *Bodily Resurrection*, 124, notes that the pre-Pauline formula includes the reference to the third day (which was the first day of the week); this reference probably reflects the events surrounding the empty tomb. Moloney, *Resurrection*, 143, maintains that there is a pre-Gospel tradition before Mark and John "with roots in solid historical memory".

14   Brown, *Bodily Resurrection*, 108–109, presents this as a "*hypothesis* which has gained a certain favour among critical scholars." See Pagola, *Jesus*, 387. Jesus mentions this on the way to Gethsemane (Mark 14:28); see also John 16:32. The Markan young man at the tomb says: "Go, tell his disciples and Peter that he is going ahead of you to Galilee; there you will see him just as he told you" (16:7). The same is true of the angel at the tomb in Matthew, and then of Jesus himself (28:7; 28:10). Lohfink, *Jesus of Nazareth*, 289, maintains that lived history lies behind these words.

15   Lohfink, *Jesus of Nazareth*, 290. As O'Collins, *Easter Jesus*, 31, points out, the disciples were crushed; they were not feverishly awaiting Jesus' return; they did not create his return out of their excited imagination.

16   Lohfink, *Jesus of Nazareth*, 298; see Dunn, *Jesus Remembered*, 834, n. 36. On pp. 842–843, considering the two accounts of appearances to women (Magdalene in John, Magdalene and others in Matthew), he asks why the evangelists accord the first appearances to women, and why Matthew includes it at all, since its purpose seems to reinforce the message given by the angels concerning Galilee. The explanation is that "there was a persistent report within the communal memory of the earliest churches that the first witnesses had been women", which Matthew could not ignore. John was in touch with an early memory that Mary of Magdala was the first to see Jesus. On p.865, he writes: "an appearance to women at or near the tomb has similar tradition-history plausibility as the account of the discovery that the tomb was empty."

17   1 Corinthians 15:3–5; Luke 24:34 (a formulaic reference); John 21:1–14. Brown, *Bodily Resurrection*, 109, suggests that Jesus appeared to Peter at the lakeside, and later to the Twelve at a meal. The glorified Lord poured out his Spirit on them and commissioned them. The implications of Jesus' resurrection gradually became evident and came to be incorporated in the narratives. O'Collins, *Easter Jesus*, 29, upholds the plausibility of the view that the disciples' encounters with Christ took place in Galilee. The disciples learned of the empty tomb only after their return to Jerusalem. Dunn, *Jesus Remembered*, 844–846, notes that Peter is the first in Paul's

list of appearances; in Luke, after the return of the Emmaus disciples, the confession of the eleven concerning Peter is given pride of place. Both Paul and Luke seem to have suppressed reports concerning the women, an understandable move, given the low esteem for women as witnesses. Considering the story in John 21, he suggests that throughout Peter's life the appearance to Peter was retained as personal testimony and never allowed to become church tradition as such. It was only after his death that is was told, with a Johannine perspective.

18   The appearances, not the empty tomb, gave rise to resurrection faith. Lohfink, *Jesus of Nazareth*, 290–91, states clearly that the appearances to Peter and the inner group of disciples took place in Galilee. Luke and John locate the appearances in Jerusalem for theological reasons. Brown, *Bodily Resurrection*, 106, rejects the harmonising possibility that Jesus appears several times to the Twelve, first in Jerusalem and then in Galilee. The different Gospel accounts are narrating the same basic appearance, whether they locate it in Jerusalem or Galilee. On p.109, he suggests that Jesus appeared to Peter on the shore of the lake, and resurrection faith was born; then he appeared to the 'Twelve', confirming the perhaps inchoate faith stirred by Peter's report. Lohfink, *Jesus of Nazareth*, 292, suggests that the high regard for Peter and his leading role in the early Church rested, among other things, on that appearance. Dodd, *Founder*, 176, observes that the disciples were sure they had met with Jesus, and there was no more to be said about it. Something changed these men; they said it was a meeting with Jesus. The nature of this meeting we cannot pretend to know. We are dealing with a truly 'historic' event.

19   "Let himself be seen" or "made himself visible" is probably a better translation than "appeared".

20   Lohfink, *Jesus of Nazareth*, 298, maintains that the disciples expected the end–time events to occur in Jerusalem.

21   Brown, *Bodily Resurrection,* 110, refers to a charismatic manifestation of the Spirit they had already received. Lohfink, *Jesus of Nazareth*, 303, stresses the eschatological dimension of this outpouring; an outpouring of the Spirit was an element of end-time expectation (Joel 2:28; 3:1–5). Earlier he stresses the link between the resurrection of Jesus and the expectations of end-time general resurrection; eschatology was strong in that first group; that is why they returned to Jerusalem, which would be the centre for end-time events.

22   See Rowan Williams, *God with Us,* 62; Chapter 2 of this book, nn. 13, 15, 34. O'Collins, *Easter Jesus,* 31, notes the current expectation that the end of the world would bring a resurrection of all the dead along with a general judgement. "Neither the disciples nor anyone else expected the resurrection of one person alone." This is something new and original. Lohfink, *Is This All There Is?* 123, notes the way in which the earliest Church called Christ "the first fruits of those who have died" (1 Cor 15:20, 23), "the firstborn among many sisters and brothers" (Rom 8:29), "the

firstborn from the dead" (Col 1:18). This shows the bond between the resurrection of Jesus and that of all the dead (1 Thess 4:14).

23   Acts 2:14–41; 3:12–26; 4:9–12; 5:29–32; 10:34–43; and Paul in 13:16–47. Luke is the author of these speeches, taking up earlier material; it gives an idea of how the first Christians proclaimed their faith, the sort of thing they were saying.

24   In 1 Corinthians 15:5–8, Paul lists others to whom the risen and glorified Jesus appeared: five hundred brothers and sisters; James; the apostles; and lastly to himself. Dodd, *Founder*, 174, notes that for Paul these appearances are facts, stemming from a date very close to the events, a particular series of occurrences, unique in character, unrepeatable and confined to a limited period. Schneiders, *Jesus Risen*, 12, observes that the data about the appearances is extensive and diverse; we are not dealing with a single, private experience. "We are dealing with something that 'happened', whatever that was or means." Dunn, *Jesus Remembered*, 858–862, lists as common elements of the core tradition: seeing, failure to recognise, commission, meal context, first day of the week; the first, third and fifth of these particularly. "No one who has studied the data can doubt that the Christian witness on this theme began from a number of experiences understood as seeings of Jesus alive after he had been dead." The stories were remembered as visual or visionary experiences, because that is how they were experienced. "That was the impact crystallised in the core tradition." They were experiences of personal encounter and communication. He concludes: "What we should recognise as beyond reasonable doubt is that the first believers experienced 'resurrection experiences' and that those experiences are enshrined, as with the earlier impact made by Jesus' teaching and actions, in the traditions which have come down to us."

25   See Rom 6:9–10. Brown, *Bodily Resurrection*. 87, speaks of the continuity of the corporeal element of personal existence. Schneiders, *Jesus Risen*, 14, writes that "we are dealing with historical experience (that of the disciples) of nonhistorical reality (the glorified Jesus) somehow mediated by body (which is what we mean by the Risen Jesus)." Lohfink, *Jesus of Nazareth*, 295–97, notes that ideas of exaltation, rapture/translation, resurrection, were already available in Jewish thought (Isa 52:13–15 and Psa 110; 2 Kgs 2:1–18; Isa 26:19 and Dan 12:2). All three are used in the early Church for Jesus; see also Brown, *Bodily Resurrection*, 76. Resurrection was understood as an eschatological event, and was for many (or all). Probably, the disciples understood Jesus' resurrection (as an individual) as introducing the general resurrection as a kind of prelude and expected this rather soon ("firstborn": 1 Cor 15:20; Col 1:18; Rev 1:5). Brown, *Bodily Resurrection*, 76, notes that the choice of resurrection language was not inevitable; there was no expectation of the raising of a single individual.

26   Williams, *God with Us*, 65.

27   Benedict XVI, *Jesus of Nazareth*, 2:244–246; on p. 266, he refers to

138

the dialectic of identity and otherness, of real physicality and freedom from the constraints of the body.

28   Pagola, *Jesus*, 392.

29   Jesus is raised by the *power* of God (2 Cor 13:4; Eph 1:19–20); by the *glory* of God (Rom 6:4; Phil 3:21); and by the *spirit* of God (Rom 8:11; 1 Cor 15:35–49). See Pagola, *Jesus*, 393–94; in n. 22, he observes that the event of the resurrection is 'real', in that it really happened, but not 'historical', in the sense that it cannot be empirically verified.

30   "See" is found in Matt 28:17, and several times in John (20:18, 20, 25, 27, 29). For "appeared" or "showed himself" see John 21:1, 14; Luke 24:34. However, the initiative always lies with Jesus who allows himself to be seen. Neutral observers would not have seen anything. Schneiders, *Jesus Risen*, 13, notes that "Those who saw the Risen Jesus knew that whatever 'seeing' meant, it was not a purely biological, optical event in the natural order, i.e., within the arena of historical cause and effect and governed by the coordinates of space and time." Dunn, *Jesus Remembered*, 872–74, comments that the passive form of the verb suggests that there was something to be seen, and what they saw was given them to see. In *Jesus and the Spirit*, (London: SCM Press, 1975), 108, he writes that Paul himself was convinced that what he saw was external to him—was Jesus alive from the dead, alive in a new mode of existence (spiritual body). Brown, *Bodily Resurrection*, 113, states that "the appearances entail a sight that involves revelation, a sight that goes beyond ordinary experience." Sight leads to insight. Moloney, *Resurrection*, 147, believes that it is impossible to describe "what happened" in the appearances in any concrete sense. Dodd, *Founder*, 174–75, comments that the occurrences were elusive, evanescent, yet "they left in the minds of those to whom they happened an unshakable conviction that they had, indeed, for a short space of time, been in the direct presence of their living Lord."

31   Moloney, *Resurrection*, 147, states that "the witness of the earliest Church that Jesus 'appeared' is firm." The reality of the experience should not be questioned. The fact that we are dealing with the action of God, God's breaking into the human realm, means that it is impossible for us to determine what really happened or adequately describe it in human language. Schneiders, *Jesus Risen*, 13, points out that the appearances were not self-induced or hallucinatory, but real, their cause being independent of the experiencing subject. They were not night visions or ecstatic events but happened when their subjects were fully awake and occupied in ordinary things.

32   O'Collins, *Easter Faith*, 25, holds that historical authenticity can hardly be claimed for any words attributed to the risen Christ. See also Wright, *The Resurrection*, 679; Pagola, *Jesus*, 401, n.49. Brown, *Bodily Resurrection*, 106–08, suggests that the various evangelists are describing the same basic appearance to the Twelve, through which they are commissioned for their future task. The words of commissioning reflect the style of the individual evangelist. Probably the risen Jesus did not use words at all. "Perhaps the category of "speaking" *may* be inadequate to

describe the unique and eschatological encounter with the Risen Jesus." There was communication; "speaking" seems to be the approximation in ordinary experience that best describes the extraordinary and indescribable.

33   Moloney, *Resurrection*, 148, concludes that there is objective evidence that the earliest Church came into existence because of the encounter with the risen Jesus–whatever that means.

34   Brown, *Bodily Resurrection*, 85–92. On p.85, n. 145, he refers to a corporeal resurrection in which the risen body is transformed to the eschatological sphere, no longer bound by space and time—a body that no longer has all the natural or physical characteristics that marked its temporal existence. For a thorough study of Paul's conversion experience, with its two elements of an appearance and an apostolic commissioning, see Dunn, *Jesus and the Spirit*, 95–122.

35   1 Cor 15:8–11; 9:1; Gal 1:13–23; Phil 3:5–14. Brown, *Bodily Resurrection*, 87, notes that Paul does not agree with Luke! On p. 89, he refers to "the artistry of effective narration" and suggests that the Gospel stories may use too broad a brush stroke in trying to capture in a narrative such a basically indescribable eschatological reality. Benedict XVI, *Jesus of Nazareth*, 2, 269, refers to Luke exaggerating in his apostolic zeal.

36   Brown, *Bodily Resurrection*, 125. The full text is found in the English edition of *L'Osservatore Romano*, April 13, 1972. For a deep and thought-provoking exploration of the meaning of bodily resurrection, see Schneiders, *Jesus Risen*, 3–33. She maintains that what is being affirmed in the New Testament material on resurrection about Jesus is not the physicality of the risen body, about which the texts are extremely discreet and even ambiguous, but the fact and the significance of Jesus' mode of presence among his disciples, a mode of presence that can only be affirmed in terms of body. Jesus was recognised as identically the same person whom the disciples had known in his earthly, pre-Easter life. He was a distinct person, distinct from them and everything else, whose presence and absence they did not control. While he was present with them, the disciples could interact with him. They did not imagine that he was present. The disciples experienced themselves as having in common their relationship with him in the present, and not merely a shared memory of his having been with them in the past. She explores the relationship between bodiliness, materiality and physicality, suggesting that bodiliness is not necessarily physical, and sees body as the symbol or symbolic presence of the self. It is the perceptible material through which the person is one-in-himself/herself, distinct from others, intersubjectively available and able to be interpersonally involved with a plurality of other selves, who are related to each other because of their relation to the one symbolised. It has to be perceptible; perceptibility (and therefore materiality) of some kind is intrinsic to symbolisation. It renders present and available what it symbolises. The body of the risen Jesus functions symbolically as his earthly body did, but the difference lies in the character, not the fact, of his bodiliness, the mode of the bodily or symbolic presence of Jesus among his disciples. For the glorified

140

Jesus, to be 'bodily' is to be personally and identically (i.e. numerically) himself in the full integrity of his humanity and able to be present and active in relation to us in whatever ways are appropriate or necessary for us.

37   The translation of Nicholas King, *The New Testament* (Stowmarket: Kevin Mayhew, 2004), 255.

38   Moloney, *Resurrection*, 154–157, notes how throughout the Gospel Jesus avoids public proclamation of his Messiahship, accepting it only in the passion (Mark 14:61–62), similarly with the title 'King of the Jews' (15:2). It is on the cross that Jesus is Messiah and King (15:31–32). The Resurrection Narrative does not explicitly proclaim the risen Jesus as the Messiah, "but there is much in the Christology of the story as a whole that points in that direction." Likewise, there is no immediate association with messianic claims in Matthew's narrative. The Lukan story concentrates on the necessity both of Jesus' death and his resurrection (27:4, 25–27). "Thus, it is written that the Christ should suffer and on the third day rise from the dead." For Luke, "Jesus' messianic status is established by means of Jesus' death and resurrection. They fulfil Jesus' promises and bring to completion the definite plan and foreknowledge of God, revealed in the scriptures." In John, Jesus resists attempts to proclaim him as messiah or king. In the "hour" he is proclaimed "King". He is established as the Christ only by fulfilling the task given him by the Father. The evangelist concludes by stating that he has told Jesus' story so that his readers and listeners "may believe in the name of Jesus, the Christ, the Son of God, and thus have life in his name" (20:30–31).

39   Matthew emphasises the Lordship of Jesus, for "all authority in heaven and on earth has been given to me." Moloney, *Resurrection*, 155, comments: "It is as Lord that the risen Jesus will be with his followers to the close of the age." John uses the term 'Lord' frequently across chapters 20–21.

40   See John V. Taylor, *A Matter of Life and Death* (London: SCM Press, 1986), 51–65.

41   Pagola, *Jesus*, 394; see 1 Cor 15:20; 1 Cor 6:14.

42   Taylor, *A Matter of Life and Death*, is my inspiration in what follows.

43   Virgil, *Aeneid*, I, line 462.

44   Jon Sobrino, *Christology at the Crossroads* (London: SCM, 1978), 158–176, suggests that God's will is that we become aware of what love demands and seek to respond accordingly.

45   Taylor, *A Matter of Life and Death*, 18.

46   This is the alternative translation of 7:38; the NRSV reads "out of the believer's heart shall flow rivers of living water." I believe, however, that the text refers primarily to the heart of Jesus, which makes our life-giving role possible.

Bibliography

Mark

Anderson, Hugh. *The Gospel of Mark.* London: Oliphants, 1976.

Boring, M. Eugene. *Mark. A Commentary.* NTL Louisville & London: Westminster John Knox, 2006.

Byrne, Brendan. *A Costly Freedom.* Collegeville, MN: Liturgical Press, 2008.

Culpepper, R. Alan. *Mark.* Macon: Smyth and Helwys, 2007.

Donahue, John R. and Harrington, Daniel H. *The Gospel of Mark.* Sacra Pagina 2. Collegeville, MN: Liturgical Press, 2002.

Harrington, Wilfrid. *Mark.* Dublin: Veritas, 1979.

Hooker, Morna D. *The Gospel according to St. Mark.* London: A&C Black, 1991.

Kingsbury, Jack D. *The Christology of Mark's Gospel.* Philadelphia: Fortress, 1983.

McBride, Denis. *The Gospel of Mark.* Dublin: Dominican Publications, 1996.

Malbon, Elizabeth S. *In the Company of Jesus: Characters in Mark's Gospel.* Louisville: Westminster John Knox, 2000.

Martin, George. *The Gospel according to Mark.* Chicago: Loyola, 2005.

Moloney, Francis J. *The Gospel of Mark. A Commentary.* Peabody, MA: Hendrickson, 2002.

_____. *Gospel Interpretation and Christian Life.* Adelaide: ATF Press, 2017.

Nineham, Dennis E. *St. Mark.* London: Penguin Books, 1963.

Senior, Donald. *The Passion of Jesus in the Gospel of Mark.* Wilmington, DE: Glazier, 1984.

Wright N. Tom. *Mark for Everyone.* London: SPCK, 2001.

Matthew

Beare, Francis W. *The Gospel according to Matthew.* Oxford: Blackwell, 1981.

Byrne, Brendan. *Lifting the Burden.* Collegeville, MN: Liturgical Press, 2004.

Davis, William D. and Allison, Dale C. *A Critical and Exegetical Commentary on the Gospel according to Saint Matthew.* London: T&T Clark, 2004.

Green, H. Benedict. *The Gospel according to Matthew.* London: Oxford University Press, 1975.

Hagner, Donald A. *Matthew.* [2 vols.] Word Biblical Commentary. Nashville: Nelson, 2000.

Harrington, Daniel. *The Gospel of Matthew.* Sacra Pagina 1. Collegeville, MN: Liturgical, 1991.

Hill, David. *The Gospel of Matthew.* London: Oliphants, 1972.

Luz, Ulrich. *Matthew.* [3 vols.] Minneapolis, MN: Augsburg Fortress, 2001, 2005, 2007.

Meier, John P. *Matthew.* Dublin: Veritas, 1980.

Senior, Donald. *Matthew.* Nashville: Abingdon Press, 1998.

Wright, N. Tom. *Matthew for Everyone.* [2 vols.] London: SPCK, 2002.

Luke

Byrne, Brendan. *The Hospitality of God.* Collegeville, MN: Liturgical Press, 2000.

Caird, George B. *St. Luke.* London: Pelican, 1963.

Carroll, John T. *Luke: A Commentary.* Louisville: Westminster John Knox Press, 2012.

Evans, Christopher F. *Saint Luke.* London: SCM, 1990.

Fitzmyer, Joseph A. *The Gospel according to Luke.* [2 vols.] New York: Doubleday, 1981, 1985.

Green, Joel B. *The Gospel of Luke,* NICNT. Cambridge: Eerdmans, 1997.

Johnson, Luke T. *The Gospel of Luke,* Sacra Pagina 3. Collegeville, MN: Liturgical Press, 1991.

Karris, Robert J. *Luke: Artist and Theologian.* New York: Paulist, 1985.

_____, 'God's Boundary-Breaking Mercy', *The Bible Today* 24, 1986.

LaVerdiere, Eugene. *Luke.* Dublin: Veritas, 1980.

Marshall, I. Howard. *The Gospel of Luke.* Exeter: Paternoster Press, 1978.

McBride, Denis. *The Gospel of Luke.* Dublin: Dominican Publications, 1991.

Tannehill, Robert C. *Luke.* Nashville: Abingdon Press, 1996.

Thompson, G.H.P. *The Gospel according to Luke.* Oxford: Clarendon Press, 1972.

Wright, N. Tom. *Luke for Everyone.* London: SPCK, 2001.

John

Barrett, C. Kingsley. *The Gospel according to John.* (2nd ed.) London: SPCK, 1978.

Brown, Raymond E., *The Gospel according to John.* [2 vols.] London: Chapmans, 1972.

Bultmann, Rudolf. *Theology of the New Testament.* Translated by Kendrick Grobel. [2 vols.] London: SCM Press, 1955.

Byrne, Brendan. *Life Abounding.* Strathfiled NSW: St Pauls Publications, 2014.

Carter, Warren. *John: Storyteller, Interpreter, Evangelist.* Peabody, MA: Hendrickson, 2006.

Chennattu, Rekha M. *Johannine Discipleship as a Covenant Relationship.* Peabody MA: Hendrickson, 2006.

Collins, Raymond F. 'Blessed are those who have not Seen: John 20:29', in Rekha M. Chennattu and Mary L Coloe. *Transcending Boundaries. Contemporary Readings of the New Testament. Essays in Honour of Francis J. Moloney.* Rome: LAS, 2005.

Coloe Mary L. *Dwelling in the Household of God.* Collegeville, MN: Liturgical Press, 2007.

Culpepper, R. Alan. *Anatomy of the Fourth Gospel*. Philadelphia: Fortress, 1983.

_____. *The Gospel and Letters of John*. Nashville: Abingdon, 1998.

Dodd, Charles H. *The Interpretation of the Fourth Gospel*. Cambridge: CUP, 1968.

Koester, Craig R. *Symbolism in the Fourth Gospel*. Minneapolis: Fortress, 2003.

_____. *The Word of Life*. Grand Rapids, MI: Eerdmans, 2008.

Lee, Dorothy A. *The Symbolic Narratives of the Fourth Gospel*. Sheffield: JSOT, 1994.

_____. *Flesh and Glory*. New York: Crossroad, 2002.

Lincoln, Andrew T. *The Gospel according to Saint John*. Grand Rapids, MI: Baker Academic, 2005.

Lindars, Barnabas. *The Gospel of John*. London: Oliphants, 1972.

Moloney, Francis J. *The Gospel of John*. Sacra Pagina 4. Collegeville, MN: Glazier, 1998.

_____. *The Gospel of John, Text and Context*. Boston: Brill, 2005.

_____. *Love in the Gospel of John*. Grand Rapids, MI: Baker Academic, 2013.

_____. *Johannine Studies 1975–2017*. Tübingen: Mohr Siebeck, 2017.

De la Potterie, Ignace. *The Hour of Jesus*. Slough: St. Pauls Press, 1989.

Schnackenburg, Rudolf. *The Gospel according to St. John*, [3 vols.] London: Burns & Oates, 1968, 1980, 1982.

Senior, Donald. *The Passion of Jesus in the Gospel of John*. Leominster: Gracewing, 1991.

Schneiders, Sandra M. *Written That You May Believe*. New York: Crossroad, 1999.

_____. *Jesus Risen in our Midst*. Collegeville, MN: Liturgical Press, 2013.

_____. 'The Resurrection (of the Body) in the Fourth Gospel: A Key to Johannine Spirituality', in Donahue John R. (ed.) *Life in Abundance Studies of John's Gospel in Tribute to Raymond E. Brown*. Collegeville, MN: Liturgical Press, 2005.

Winstanley, Michael T. *Symbols and Spirituality*. Bolton: Don Bosco Publications, 2007.

Other Books

Bailey, Kenneth E. *The Good Shepherd*. London: SPCK, 2015.

Benedict XVI. *Jesus of Nazareth*, [2 vols.] London: Bloomsbury, 2007; San Francisco: Ignatius Press, 2011.

Brown, Raymond E. *The Virginal Conception and Bodily Resurrection of Jesus*. London: Geoffrey Chapman, 1974.

_____. *The Death of the Messiah*, [2 vols.] London: Geoffrey Chapman, 1994.

_____. *An Introduction to the New Testament*. The Anchor Bible Reference Library. New York: Doubleday, 1997.

_____. *A Risen Christ in Eastertime*. Collegeville, MN; Liturgical Press, 1991.

Dodd, Chares H. *The Founder of Christianity*. London: Fontana, 1971.

Dunn, James D.G. *Jesus Remembered*. Cambridge, Eerdmans, 2003.

_____. *A New Perspective*. London: SPCK, 2005.

Evans, Christopher F. *Resurrection and the New Testament*. London: SCM, 1970.

Fuller, Reginald H. *The Formation of the Resurrection Narratives*. London: SPCK, 1972.

Lohfink, Gerhard. *Jesus of Nazareth. What He wanted. Who He was* Translated by Linda M. Maloney. Collegeville, MN: Liturgical Press, 2012.

_____. *Is This All There Is? On Resurrection and Eternal Life*. Translated by Linda M. Maloney. Collegeville, MN: Liturgical Press, 2017.

Moloney, Francis J. *The Resurrection of the Messiah*. New York: Paulist Press, 2013;

_____. *The Gospel of Mark*. Peabody, MA: Hendrickson, 2002.

_____. *A Body Broken for a Broken People. Marriage, Divorce, and the Eucharist*. Mulgrave: Garratt, 2015.

_____. *Reading the New Testament in the Church. A Primer for Pastors, Religious Educators, and Believers*. Grand Rapids, MI: Baker Academic, 2015.

Nouwen, Henri J. M. *With Open Hands*. Notre Dame Indiana: Ave Maria Press, 1972.

O'Collins, Gerald. *The Easter Jesus.* London: DLT, 1973.

_____, *Easter Faith.* London: DLT, 2003.

Pagola, José A. *Jesus, An Historical Approximation.* Miami: Convivium, 2011.

Perrin, Norman. *The Resurrection Narratives. A New Approach.* London: SCM, 1997.

Sobrino, Jon. *Christology at the Crossroads.* London: SCM, 1978.

Williams, Rowan. *Resurrection.* London: DLT, 2014 (3rd ed.).

_____. *God with Us.* London: SPCK, 2017.

Rigaux, Beda. *Dio l'ha risuscitato.* Milano: Edizioni Paoline, 1976.

Taylor, John V. *A Matter of Life and Death.* London: SCM, 1986.

Winstanley, Michael T. *Come and See.* London: DLT, 1985.

_____. *Jesus and the Little People.* Bolton: Don Bosco Publications, 2012.

Wright, N. Tom. *Jesus and the Victory of God.* London: SPCK, 2000.

_____. *The Resurrection of the Son of God.* London: SPCK, 2003.

Other books by
Michael T. Winstanley SDB

An Advent Journey. Bolton: Don Bosco Publications, 2014.

Come and See. London: Darton, Longman and Todd, 1985.

Don Bosco's Gospel Way. Bolton: Don Bosco Publications, 2002.

Into Your Hands. Homebush, NSW: St Paul's Publications, 1994.

Jesus and the Little People. Bolton: Don Bosco Publications, 2012.

Lenten Sundays. Bolton: Don Bosco Publications, 2011.

Scripture, Sacraments, Sprituality. Essex: McCrimmon Publishing Co. Ltd., 2002.

Symbols and Spirituality. Bolton: Don Bosco Publications, 2007.

Walking with Luke: Thematic Studies in the Lukan Narative with Reflections Bolton: Don Bosco Publications, 2017.

About the Author

Michael T. Winstanley is a Salesian of Don Bosco. He is a graduate of the Salesian Pontifical University, Rome, and London University. He lectured in biblical studies at Ushaw College, Durham, for seventeen years. Michael has spent many years in Formation Ministry, served twice as Provincial of the British Province, given retreats in many countries and been involved in a variety of adult education programmes. For twelve years, he worked with the Salesian volunteers at Savio Retreat House in Bollington. Currently, he is Vicar for Religious in the Salford Diocese. This is his tenth book.